Is your child safe online?

A parent's guide to the internet,
Facebook, mobile phones &
other new media

Pamela Whitby

white
LADDER

Is your child safe online? A parent's guide to the internet, Facebook, mobile phones and other new media

This first edition published in 2011 by Crimson Publishing, a
division of Crimson Business Ltd, Westminster House, Kew Road,
Richmond, Surrey TW9 2ND

© Pamela Whitby 2011

The right of Pamela Whitby to be identified as the author of this
work has been asserted by her in accordance with the Copyright,
Designs and Patents Act, 1988.

British Library Cataloguing in Publication Data
A catalogue record for this book is available from the British Library

ISBN 978 1 90541 094 1

Designed by Andy Prior
Typeset by IDSUK (DataConnection) Ltd
Printed and bound in Italy by LegoPrint SpA, Trento

Contents

Contents

Acknowledgements

This book would not have been possible without the input of a number of people. Thank you to all who generously gave their time to share stories, insights, expertise and research, who responded to countless email queries and even read chunks of the text for factual accuracy, content and readability.

They are: Shirley Atkinson, Lance Bellers, Hannah Bickers, Teresa Bliss, Christopher Boyd, John Carr, Yvonne Chapman, Sarah Crouch, Rik Ferguson, Shane Gallagher, Will Gardner, Mark Griffiths, Kate Hamshar, Mike Hawkes, Linda Hillier, Graham Jones, Martina Jones, Chloe Kelly-O'Meara, Adam Liversage, Sonia Livingstone, Elena Martellozzo, Marian Merritt, Dave Miles, Marie T Molinet, Rebecca Newton, Alana O'Sullivan, Maureen O'Sullivan, Sean Richardson, Tim Riches, Jérôme Valette, William Webb, Kate Wilson, Clint Witchalls.

I am particularly indebted to Basil Lawrence for his detailed page edit and illuminating suggestions and insights and Dave Miles for reading the book and his cover quote.

For obvious reasons, there are also a number of people who prefer to remain anonymous. A huge thank you to all of you for providing the diverse human backdrop that makes this such a fascinating subject. In particular I would like to thank all the children and teenagers who took part.

Thanks also to Beth Bishop at Crimson Publishing for her support.

Finally, I must thank my children, Neve and Calum, for testing some of the technology and for putting up with a grumpy Mum when the early starts got too much. I hope what I have learnt benefits them. And finally, thanks to my lovely husband Fergus Clegg for wholeheartedly supporting my decision to take on what has been a very interesting and rewarding project.

Introduction

Can you remember a time when a mobile was for telephone calls and texting, a computer was a glorified typewriter and tweeting was what birds did on a spring morning? It was not that long ago. But new developments in technology are happening daily and are radically altering the world we live in and the way we interact with each other. Such forces are changing the face of business, education and society forever and are sweeping the emerging generation – our children – along with them.

Technology is now an integral part of our children's lives and it is here to stay. Globally there are 84 million under-17s online each day. And closer to home the popularity of our webbed world is growing apace. Only a few years ago, the average age for a child in the UK to begin accessing the internet was nine. Today they are as young as five.

Herein lies the big issue: how much do parents really know about this new generation of technology? We hear stories in the media of cyber-bullying, the early sexualisation of childhood, of predatory paedophiles, and the ills of social networking.

But do we know how our own children are using this technology? More importantly, are *we* doing enough to keep them safe?

It dawned on me that the only way to tackle this complicated subject would be to talk directly with children. I started by interviewing a group of 17-year-olds. My admittedly unscientific thinking was that if they – the first survivors of the so-called 'screenager generation' – were willing to talk, they would know better than anybody what parents today should be worrying about.

A friend's teenage daughter agreed to rope in some friends and one afternoon an intelligent, diverse and internet-savvy crowd shared their views with me. By the end of three exhausting, enlightening (and at times shocking) hours I felt I had heard – and seen – it all.

They regaled me with some pretty grim stories of cyber-bullying taken to extremes and Facebook postings gone horribly wrong. Together we logged onto Chatroulette, an eye-popping website where men and women – and even apparently unmonitored children claiming to be 12 years old – use webcam with live chat where some even expose themselves. I was introduced to 'fraping', or Facebook raping, and shown that YouTube works as a social network.

If that was not enough to take on board, they saddened me by describing how easy access to pornography puts pressure on their relationships, body image and self-esteem and how worried they were about the rise of pro-anorexia and bulimia websites. While these children clearly love using technology – and their lives depend on it – they recognise it isn't all good.

So what would be their top tips for parents? The answer seemed wise beyond their years.

> *"Talk to, but more importantly listen to, your children, give them freedom but have boundaries too, and be careful with your credit card."*
> **Advice from teenagers**

Since that afternoon I have interviewed a wide range of people, from internet and educational psychologists to teachers, IT professionals, academics, criminologists, industry representatives and, yes, more children in the five to 16 age range. What they all (perhaps bar some of the children) seem to unequivocally agree on is this: communicating with your child about online safety is the most powerful and effective tool we parents have.

FACT One in four children still think they know more about the internet than their parents.
Nearly half of UK parents do not have any filtering or monitoring software installed on their computers.[1]

We parents also seem to want to believe in our children's innocence. The same research finds that of the children who admitted to seeing sexual images online, 40% of their parents said they had not. When it came to children who had met an online stranger offline, 61% of parents did not believe it.

Where does this leave parents?

It leaves us in a world changing at eye-watering speeds, where ever younger children are accessing the internet and where new risks are emerging all the time. Aside from the social risks such as cyber-bullying and the commercial risks such as online identity theft, there are other potential ticking time bombs. Among these are the early sexualisation of childhood, the threat of user-generated content (pro-anorexia, bulimia and self-harm websites), addiction to screens and the possibility that internet use could be changing the way our children think. The impact of all these on society is not yet clear and may not be for some time to come.

There are, however, so many positive opportunities that new technology has created – such as creating, editing and uploading videos, blogging to improve literacy, gaming for maths skills (see p115) – that are very often overshadowed by the darker side.

There is a strong argument to suggest that the biggest risk of all is that some of our children may be missing out on the benefits of new technology because of our own fears or lack of understanding about how our children are using it.

On this level we need more research; we need to understand more. And we parents need to consider what we should be asking from government, industry and, indeed, technology (see Part 4).

What is certain, too, is that our older children have moved on somewhat from what parents perceive to be the biggest dangers of the internet; educational initiatives are starting to pay off. The problem is that while we are still worrying about them accessing pornography, the challenges have shifted. Cyber-bullying, 'sexting', posting inappropriate images and accessing websites that are not age-appropriate are the issues we need to be thinking about, and learning about, now.

No doubt my prophetic first interviewees will have a better idea of how to parent their children in the information age. But for us – the parenting generation who, rightly or wrongly, remember childhood as wind-in-hair freedom, board games and a spot of benign telly when the nights drew in – navigating the minefield of the online world is more confusing.

Let us be clear: this book cannot be a 'how to' guide to the intricacies of every technological device. Instead it is intended to help you make sense of the bigger issues facing you, and provide you with practical advice as your children hurtle ever more confidently into the information age.

Parents have always had a responsibility to guide, protect, inspire and teach their children. It has never been an easy job but, platitudes aside, it comes with the territory – and if it is not what most children want, it is what they need.

How this book is structured

This book is divided into four parts.

As much of the discussion around children using the internet starts with the subject of risks, it is necessary to get these fully in perspective. In Part 1 we look at what these risks are and why we need to be aware of them. We also dispel some of the myths surrounding the use of the internet, and help you understand exactly what risks your child may encounter. This acts as an overview; we go into detail, giving you specific practical advice, in Part 3.

Part 2 is dedicated to general advice about internet safety, such as where and how to assess safety software and what to know about your child's school's e-safety policy.

By the time you get to Part 3 you will have a clear overview of what your child may face, and be ready to learn more about what they may be doing and how you as a parent can deal with this and help them. In this section you will find plenty of case studies and experiences of teachers, children and parents, as well as advice from industry.

Part 4 looks to the future – we take a brief look at what we need to be aware of going forward and how we can play a part in the safety of our children and future generations.

Author's notes

- For the purposes of this book a 'child' is anybody under the age of 18. In the UK there is no single law that defines the age of a child across the country, but when it comes to child protection guidance, England, Wales, Northern Ireland and Scotland agree that a child is anybody who has not yet reached their 18th birthday.
- Any research is referenced in endnotes. The main reports used for statistics can be found on p169.
- For the less technology-literate, there is a jargon-busting glossary for terms not explained fully in the text.
- I have referred to a child as a boy throughout, except when specifically discussing issues related to girls only. This is for consistency and ease of reading.
- Advancements in technology are happening every day, and the online world is constantly evolving. While every effort was made to ensure that this book was accurate when going to press, please be aware that there will undoubtedly be further advancements that you may need to be aware of.

Part 1

Risks and myths – setting the record straight

In recent years there has been a high-profile publicity push to raise parents' awareness of the online risks to children. Countless organisations, from e-safety bodies to government departments, the police, research institutes and firms flogging software, have pumped out statistics that tell us what we do and do not know, and also what we *should* know, about our children's internet use.

The press have a habit of scaremongering parents and hyping the online risks to our children out of all proportion. Often articles are poorly researched and people are regularly misquoted. Numbers are bandied about which at first glance appear shocking, but dig a little deeper and you quickly start to understand what sells newspapers.

Sometimes the information we are given is contradictory and, while researchers do their best to represent a diverse cross-section of society, the reality is that most studies only manage to focus on a very small section of the population.

To make matters worse, just when we feel we are getting to grips with our child's online safety, a big story like the Sony PlayStation hacking debacle hits the headlines. If one of the biggest and most respected media companies on earth is vulnerable to a security breach leaving millions of users (including our children) around the world vulnerable to identity theft, then is anything really safe?

But the big question is – scary stories aside – are parents doing enough to protect their children online? Probably not. And can we do more? Absolutely! There certainly seems to be a gap between what we think we know about internet safety, and what we actually know.

> *"Parents are still worrying about their children accessing inappropriate content; but by far the biggest problems today are behavioural issues like cyber-bullying, 'sexting' and under-age children signing up to social networks that require children to be over 13."*
> **David Miles, director, Europe, Middle East and Africa, Family Online Safety Institute (FOSI)**

The aim of Part 1 is to bring some perspective to the risks which face our children. If we are not educated about these, we can't move forward with the confidence necessary to help our children remain safe. We also cannot make the most of what is an exciting and educational tool.

> *"The biggest problem for children is actually their parents who either tend to overestimate or underestimate the risks. Most are not doing enough to protect their child online and – much worse – are failing to help them maximise their use of the technology which is such an incredible resource."*
> **Graham Jones, internet psychologist**

So what exactly *should* we be worrying about?

The 3Cs

Most experts in the field of e-safety seem to agree that there are three or four things we need to be aware of. These have been defined by a number of organisations as the '3Cs'.[2] Depending on who is doling out the advice, these stand for:

- **contact** – with strangers, potential child abusers or bullies

- **content** – pornography, violence and so-called 'user-generated' content which can include hate messages or pro-anorexia, bulimia or self-harm websites

- **cost and commerce** – these are the commercial risks such as data collection or unwanted advertising to children, piracy or illegal downloads, malware and so on

or:

- **conduct** – encouraging responsible behaviour online by not giving out passwords and so on.

You might already be aware of some of the areas listed above (hence you bought the book); others may not have occurred to you. So before we take you through exactly how you can help your child (Parts 2 and 3), we'll inform you of what you really need to be aware of.

Some of it is pretty hard-hitting, but it is a reality of the world we live in. It is only by understanding the risks that we can take steps to protect our children. Against this backdrop, let us take a deep breath and put things in perspective.

1

External threats
Grooming and inappropriate content

Grooming

We're going to start with the thing that the vast majority of parents are most afraid of: that their child is being groomed online by a sexual offender who they later choose to meet and are sexually abused by. While this might be the most terrifying online risk, that doesn't mean to say it is the most likely. Let us start with some legal definitions and then try to make sense of what is a very complicated and uncomfortable subject.

What is grooming?

In the Sexual Offences Act of 2003 grooming is defined as: "A course of conduct enacted by a suspected paedophile, which would give a reasonable person cause for concern that any meeting with a child arising from the conduct would be for unlawful purposes."

To understand grooming, it is essential that parents understand the difference between a 'paedophile' and a 'sexual predator' – which is often misrepresented by the media. A paedophile is interested in pre-pubescent children whereas a predator is interested in post-pubescent juveniles. It is the latter that we parents need to be more concerned by.

Dr Elena Martellozzo is a criminologist at Middlesex University who has worked closely with the Metropolitan Police High Technological Crime Unit (HTCU) in observing the interaction between sex offenders and undercover police officers posing as children. In the course of her work she has become very wary of labels like 'paedophile' or 'predator'.

> *"In reality, sex offenders – the term I use – who target juveniles online are a diverse group that cannot be accurately characterised with one-dimensional labels. It is also very difficult to profile a sex offender with the objective of grooming children."*
> **Dr Elena Martellozzo, criminologist**

As Dr Martellozzo implies, grooming can take many forms; let us consider the range of characteristics of a 'groomer'.

- Groomers get children to co-operate by showing an interest as well as support and understanding of their lives.
- Groomers' online profiles may range from being very open and confident about stating their sexual preferences to hyper-cautious. Before making an approach with a child they will 'test the water' and behave in a passive manner, at least initially.
- Confident risk-takers may, as an example, openly state a 'pervy' desire for 'paedo' relations.
- Cautious types will use cartoon figures or toys as a profile picture.
- Hyper-cautious groomers are arguably the most dangerous as they will cover their tracks and are the most difficult to identify.
- This type might insist on seeing the potential victim on webcam, hearing a voice or receiving photographs before they actively begin grooming.

- Not all groomers aim to meet up with a child. Some seek images to share with other abusers.
- Some obtain images to blackmail a victim at a later date.
- Troubled children from dysfunctional families are more likely to be vulnerable to grooming. Sex offenders know this.

Make sure you are aware of what grooming entails – the practical advice provided in Parts 2 and 3 will arm you with all you need to protect your child online. That said, be realistic about this threat to your child.

How common is grooming?

A recent report by the Child Exploitation and Online Protection Centre (CEOP)[3] states that online grooming is a central and growing trend, but looking a little closer puts these figures into perspective.

There were 6,291 reports of suspected child sexual abuse between February 2009 and March 2010, 25% of which were grooming-related. The majority were reports of suspected online grooming rather than incidents that happened in the real world; evidence from police forces also suggests an increase in grooming cases. Of the 1,536 reports of suspected grooming made to CEOP:

- 28% involved inciting a child to perform a sexual act
- 25% related to suspicious contact
- 12% were about inciting a child to watch a sexual act
- 11% involved suspicious online contact with a child through social network sites
- 9% were to do with making arrangements to meet a child
- 417 reports related to Windows Live Messenger (formerly MSN)
- 166 came from Facebook
- just 55 related to offline suspicious activity.

The mere thought of child abuse is hard enough for most people to stomach, but before going any further let us put these numbers in perspective.

The UK's population is close to 62 million and around 12.5 million are under the age of 16. So if two-thirds of those are aged five to 16, then your child has less than a one in a million chance of being groomed. With 5,000 children under the age of 16 dying or being injured on the road in Britain each year,[4] road safety is arguably a bigger problem.

It is also worth bearing in mind that the rising numbers of reported cases could be down to the high-profile ClickCEOP campaign. According to a BBC report,[5] within the first month of ClickCEOP's launch, more than 200 UK Facebook users had reported suspicious behaviour, representing a seven-fold increase in cases.

What is ClickCEOP?

It is an application which appears as a small icon or button on some social networking or chat websites. It is a default setting on some sites like Bebo (the first to launch the application in November 2009) and Windows Live Messenger. In July 2010 Facebook agreed to launch the 'app' but, at the time of going to press, this remained an optional download on Facebook. If a user clicks on it they are immediately taken to a CEOP webpage offering advice, help and the option to report a potential threat.

Remember that these are reports of 'suspected' suspicious behaviour. There is also a tendency for children (and indeed adults) to automatically click a new button just to see where it takes them. Furthermore, every report of suspected child abuse must be fully investigated by the police but very often these turn out to be no more than pranks. "'Pedo38', an avatar posing as a 38-year-old, will quite often turn out to be a 12-year-old boy playing a joke on a friend. This happens all the time in this business at vast taxpayers' expense," explains Rebecca Newton, chief community and safety officer at online game developer Mind Candy.

Whether campaigns like ClickCEOP are useful or not remains a point of contention. Even CEOP admits that it is "difficult to tell whether there is an increase in such incidences or whether there is increased reporting as a result of heightened levels of awareness."[6]

> *"I am not entirely convinced of the effectiveness of ClickCEOP on social networking sites because children are very unlikely to recognise that they are being groomed or that they are in danger."*
> **Dr Elena Martellozzo, criminologist**

This is perhaps worrying when a CHILDWISE report[7] finds that most children feel confident that they would be able to recognise an imposter online. It is essential that children understand that not everybody is who they say they are. On p40 you'll find a set of tools to help you talk to your child about the dangers of meeting strangers online.

Rebecca Newton is a victim of paedophilia herself. She has been involved in e-safety in the children's online world since the 1980s. As an appointed member of several UK bodies such as the United Kingdom Council for Child Internet Safety, and the Internet Watch Foundation, she is passionate about ensuring that children are safe, and part of this means educating parents about the risks.

> *"The most important thing a parent can do is become culturally aware of how the online world really works. And this means not overreacting to the stories in the media about grooming because the truth is that 95% of what happens online is amazing, creative and wonderful."*
> **Rebecca Newton, chief community and safety officer at Mind Candy, the company behind Moshi Monsters**

This is not to say there are not risks or that we should underestimate the seriousness of predatory behaviour. Of course, this is a very complex subject, but as parents let us get one thing straight: the idea that predatory paedophiles are hiding in, or under, every virtual bush is simply not true.

The truth about porn

Ask any group of parents how they would feel if they found their teenager looking at pornography online and the responses will likely vary from 'hooray, they have a normal libido' to 'the devil is at work'. However, when your nine-year-old gets sent an inappropriate image via email, things get more serious. You don't have to search for porn any more – it comes to you. This is a very emotive and subjective area but what all of us will agree on is that the internet has made pornography more accessible.

> "In my day I'd go to the bookstore and take a look at magazines. But it would literally be a furtive glance at the top shelf. It is so easy to access pornographic content today and one of my biggest worries is this creates an unrealistic expectation of what sex is and I worry how this will impact on my kids' future sexual relationships."
> **Lyle, dad to Ned (15) and Eva (11)**

There are indeed growing concerns that children are becoming sexualised at a much younger age. Many educational psychologists have experienced a rising number of cases of inappropriate sexual conduct in secondary schools.

This could be as a result of early access to pornography on the internet. As Dr Linda Papadopoulos points out in her *Sexualisation of Young People* review,[8] there is "no 'watershed' on the internet, and sexualised images and adverts may appear anywhere and are often sent indiscriminately to email accounts and mobile phones". So even if your child doesn't want to receive it, they still might.

Research into children's exposure to or use of pornography is limited for obvious reasons; it is difficult to frame questions in such a way that protects those who may be unaware of such material. Within these constraints, the latest research shows that over a 12-month period:

- nearly a quarter of nine- to 16-year-olds had seen sexual images
- older children are more likely to have been exposed – 11% of nine- and ten-year-olds, but 39% of 15- and 16-year-olds
- these images were both offline and online
- in the UK television is a more common source of sexual imagery than the internet.[9]

Most of us instinctively – and rightly – wish to prevent our young children from exposure to violent or pornographic, or violent *and* pornographic, images. We also wish for our children to develop a healthy sexuality and form positive sexual relationships. This is all part of growing up and enjoying life.

> *"I've caught my 14-year-old looking at porn a few times. I remember the boys I went to secondary school with were all looking at porn mags at his age so while I am keen for him not to be made to feel like a pervert for showing an interest in sex, I also don't want him looking at hardcore porn and getting a wrong impression of a loving relationship."*
> **Barbara, mum to Dan (14) and James (11)**

Parents rightly worry about the impact of sexualised images on their children's future relationships. Research in the Netherlands[10] suggests that young people's lack of sexual experience, emotional immaturity and inability to critically appraise material could lead them to view sexually explicit material online as the 'norm'. This seems to be the experience of many children.

> *"I think porn gives boys a really unrealistic image of what sex is about. Some are really addicted to it. They watch it constantly."*
> **Alice, 16**

> *"At my school boys talk about girls in a really horrible way. They say what they prefer in girls and it is always very pornographic."*
> **Ahmed, 16**

"If we are not like that, we are outcasts in a way sometimes. I feel the way any porn is done is always really degrading to women. Even if you cover up and stuff, you get called frigid. You are either frigid or you are a slag."
Caroline, 16

So, how do we deal with this? Is government intervention needed and should internet service providers be forced to take more responsibility? While the powers that be battle it out, it is essential that the lines of communication between parents and children are kept open. One way of doing this is to open a discussion about how pornography can negatively impact on the people involved in it.

For example, talk frankly in a matter-of-fact way about how porn can objectify women and how some people are forced into this multi-billion-dollar industry because they have no choice.

While this chapter may have covered your worst fears, and understandably so, the issues raised are not actually the most likely safety concerns our children face online. Believe it or not, the most common risks to their health and safety actually stem from the children themselves.

The risks coming from children themselves

The rise in risk-taking behaviour

While the grooming of young children online is very rare, the rise of what CEOP calls 'risk-taking behaviour' by older children is a more worrying trend. In picking up this book, your main concern may have been the risk of grooming, but most experts now agree that the much bigger risk your child faces comes from themselves. Certainly topping the list of priorities for CEOP this year will be children who are putting themselves at risk.[11]

> *"There seems to be a rise in such behaviour especially by young girls with some presenting themselves as much older than they actually are."*
> **Dr Elena Martellozzo, criminologist**

Risk-taking behaviour could be anything from posting provocative photographs of themselves or comments on social networking sites, sending sexual images of themselves or messages ('sexts'; see p147) to others by mobile, to engaging in sexual activity in webcam-based chat rooms. It could also be sharing too much personal information, like names and addresses or passwords, with people they know very little about. In this regard, the rising number of webcam-streaming chat sites is a growing concern.

> "CEOP's image analysis and victim identification team has identified girls as young as eight carrying out sexual acts on webcam through chat rooms."[12]
> **Child Exploitation and Online Protection Centre**

Websites with chat rooms tend to appeal to the interests of young children so rising predatory activity on these is a concern. CEOP warns that they create opportunities for sexual predators, who sometimes use video capture software to record video streams that can be viewed or sold on for profit at a later date.

Chatroulette is one of these countless webcam-based chat services. Launched by a 17-year-old Russian to pair random strangers anywhere in the world for live conversation using webcam and a microphone, the service quickly became known for its X-rated content. It requires you to be over 18 but many teenagers lie about their age.

Age restrictions are meaningless

Debbie and Elena, 16, logged on to Chatroulette as a joke. "We had heard about it at school and were curious to find out what it was about," says Debbie. The two girls logged in to the site which is, supposedly, restricted to over-18s. "It was hilarious," says Elena. "There were all these gross old men sitting there at their desk or on their beds waiting to chat to us. Some of them started flashing us. Then these two young kids came on and we asked them how old they were. They said 12 and they looked it. They started saying things like 'show us your tits'."

Cyber-bullying – and its younger brother, cyber-aggression

So your child has not been punched in the playground or followed by an abusive gang of teenagers down to the local park. But yesterday, his phone bleeped and as he read the message you saw his face instantly pale. A few hours later the phone went again, this time over dinner. You wonder why he seems to have instantly lost his appetite. Later your sleep is disturbed by his phone bleeping again, and again, and again. What on earth is going on? Well, the bully is no longer in the park: it is in his pocket – and it is making your child very unhappy.

This sort of scenario is increasingly common in secondary schools and we need to take it very seriously, as it is something our children worry about most. But what is going on? Well, your child is being bullied and let us be clear: cyber-bullying is bullying. There is an intention to hurt, an imbalance of power, it happens repeatedly and the victims are unable to defend themselves. The 'cyber' bit relates to where and how the bullying happens – in other words, it is conveyed by some electronic medium, be that a mobile phone, blog, online chat room or social networking site.

Because this is arguably one of the biggest issues facing us as parents and our children today, it is a theme that runs throughout the book. In this section we have flagged up the risk but in Part 2 we look at how you can actively stop cyber-bullying – and what to do if your child is actually the bully.

In Part 3 there are some examples of how cyber-bullying manifests itself in new social media like Facebook (Chapter 11) and on websites like Little Gossip (p77) and Formspring (p134).

Cybersex – you had better believe it

Parents may not want to believe it – and when they are told they often don't – but cybersex (a virtual sexual encounter between two or more people) happens. And it occurs not only with teenagers, but with younger children too.

E-safety professionals say that more often than not, if you ring parents to tell them their children have been involved in cybersex, the response will be: 'No way, my child would never do that.'

Cybersex is perhaps not surprising. Children are sexual beings and in the course of growing up have probably always, to some degree or other, explored their bodies and sexuality. In our day this would have taken the form of 'doctors and nurses'-type games. So this could be viewed as another manifestation of real-world activities happening online because that is where many children now spend their time.

However, while what Mind Candy's Rebecca Newton describes as "harmless cybersex or doctor-doctor" is sometimes seen on websites like Moshi Monsters (which leads to immediate suspension of the account and parents being notified), it can be much more than that. Every hour of the day, she says, e-safety professionals see children prostituting (engaging in cybersex) themselves in exchange for virtual goods – whatever the currency is on a site, such as clothes, room items or gold.

Harmless or not, cybersex is a reality of our online world and, for obvious reasons, places children at risk. One of these reasons is that the internet has made the easy distribution of content very straightforward.

CEOP offers this warning: "The threat posed by those who sexually abuse and exploit children remains at a significant level. The threat is particularly prevalent when it focuses on those who are most vulnerable and it adapts and changes according to the availability of the children in the converged environment and the ability to exploit technology."

The key word here is 'vulnerable'. "This is the kid who has never had a boyfriend or whose parents are never at home and show no interest in them," says Newton.

This is something parents must be increasingly aware of, says CEOP, because there is evidence to suggest that with rising numbers of inappropriate self-taken images appearing on social networking sites, the nature of grooming is changing. In Chapter 6 we look at what is appropriate for your child to post and why.

User-generated content

In recent years the pressure on people to conform to a certain 'look' or 'image' has been exacerbated by a celebrity-obsessed media. Lines and wrinkles are airbrushed out of magazine photographs, cosmetic surgery is promoted as the door to happiness and ever-lasting youth, and there is a strong message driven home that thin is in.

> "If I were a parent, I'd be really worried about pro-anorexia
> websites. It is so easy to get tips online to help you stop
> eating. I did it, I should know."
> *Dan, 17*

Dan is one of a small minority of boys affected by an eating disorder. In the UK conservative estimates are that 1.1 million people have eating disorders, with young people in the age group 14–25 being most at risk. The highest rates of anorexia are seen in girls aged between 13 and 19.

Elena, 16, was affected too. "When I was in Year 9, I got loads of messages on Bebo [a social network for teens] from people I didn't know. They sent me websites like gobeanorexic.com or gokillyourself.com," she says.

It is indeed alarming that one in five teenage girls has visited a pro-anorexia or bulimia website. Other types of so-called user-generated content include hate messages, and those encouraging self-harm and experiences related to drug taking. In the UK 19% of 11- to 16-year-olds have seen one or more of these types of user-generated content, rising to 32% in the 14–16 age range.[13]

While little is known yet about the use of this content or its impact, it is something we parents need to be aware of. Helping your child to understand the messages being delivered in magazines, on television and the internet is an essential part of this.

This chapter has brought up a heap of issues that, as parents, we can actually do something about. We'll cover more of what you can do to help your child stay safe online in Part 2.

3

Consumer kids and commercial risks

While it may not be what you are most worried about, make no mistake: the biggest challenge facing our children as they navigate the online world is commercial. There is no escaping it. While grooming statistics can be reasoned away, every single child who accesses the internet comes up against commercial risks. This could be anything from running up a huge mobile bill to downloading illegal content or a malicious virus. And it's something parents need to be just as aware of as other, more sinister threats.

Exposure to advertisements

There is no such thing as an 'innocent' advert and the marketing of products to children online is a multi-billion-pound industry. It is also a big headache for parents, who are under increasing pressure from their children to buy the latest toy or device. Many well-known children's brands like Build-A-Bear, Bratz and Barbie have launched virtual worlds to extend their reach. But it also works the other way; if a brand starts life in the online world, the arrival of real-world products happens soon enough.

"I was so excited when I got my giant Puffle from Argos."
Lulu, 10 (Puffle is a character from Club Penguin)

Young children may find it difficult to distinguish between advertising and entertainment, so it is important for parents to help them understand the difference even when they are young. Part of this process means understanding the importance of online privacy because advertisers are actively gathering information on how children act online. Websites use a range of different mechanisms to do this.

Becoming familiar with some of the techniques used and understanding how websites market to children is a helpful exercise.

- **Immersive advertising** – this was first used by the children's online game Neopets (see p110) and involves the integration of advertising into a website's content. So a child plays a game about monsters, for example, but then the products of sponsors – say, a Disney trailer – are incorporated into the game.
- **Pop-ups and banner adverts** – adverts are part of recommender systems, and the artificial intelligence and algorithms that build those create a profile of the individual based on all the personal data provided. Adverts are then targeted to those individuals, which is how the likes of Google and Facebook can charge more for providing advertising space (as their adverts are more targeted).

Online fraud

As well as the impact of adverts on our children's shopping habits, we also need to worry about them using our credit card without our knowledge. In 2010 the credit card protection firm CPP talked to around a thousand children and found that one in seven were using their parents' credit card to make online purchases without their knowledge. In total this cost us around £64 million.

The research also showed that 80% of children use their parents' bank cards, online accounts and PayPal, and many do not bother to check the security of websites when shopping online. This puts us at risk from fraudsters. See p105 for clear advice on staying safe in virtual worlds.

But our children themselves could also be engaging in online fraud. Hacking may be a joke for many teenagers but it is also a criminal offence.

Downloads – the illegal and the inadvertent

"To be honest, if they are downloading music illegally, that would be one of the least of my worries."
Maureen, mum to Molly (13), Annette (9) and Eric (8)

This is certainly not what the music or entertainment industry wants to hear from parents. In 2010 Britons downloaded 1.2 billion digital music tracks and around three out of four of those were acquired illegally. While we do not know how many children are actually downloading music or films illegally, we do know that downloading music – legally or illegally – is something they love to do.

FACT Two in five 12- to 15-year-olds think that downloading shared copies of music and movies for free should not be illegal.[14]

Parents should be aware that using illegal peer-to-peer file-sharing software programmes comes with several risks, and not just legal ones.

How does peer-to-peer file sharing work?

In the broadest sense, peer-to-peer, or P2P, is a way of sharing files over the internet. If your child wants to access or share songs, films, games or any other file, then they could download an application and immediately begin accessing files that are available on another person's computer.

So, why is this problematic when file sharing *per se* is not illegal? Well, the bottom line is that any copyrighted file cannot be downloaded legally without permission of the person who owns the rights – and most of the content downloaded through P2P is being shared without permission.

> *"For one, file sharing of unauthorised, copyrighted material is illegal; two, it threatens our content and creative industries; and three, it can expose users to potentially unwanted content. You might think you are downloading a Britney Spears album but it could well be a pornographic file that has been labelled to trick you. Many of them also contain a number of malicious files like spyware or viruses. As a result you may be inadvertently disclosing personal details."*
> **Adam Liversage, director of communications at BPI, the British recorded music industry body**

Even if parents have installed software to filter out unwanted content (see p58), this is not effective when illegal services are used and this could leave children exposed. These programs can also inadvertently share personal computer files containing financial information. Quite often malicious files on these websites are given false names to trick users into downloading them.

> *"P2P was the most common method for the distribution of indecent images, closely followed by commercial websites and social networking sites."*
> **CEOP, Strategic Overview 2009–10**

Using such programs could also lead to a criminal record. If your child is consistently downloading music or entertainment illegally you could soon be receiving a warning letter from your internet service provider. If you receive three warning letters, the personal details of the account holder will be handed to the owner of the copyrighted material and you may find yourself in court.

Malicious malware – spam, viruses and other net nasties

If you have ever had to fork out hundreds of pounds to fix or replace a damaged computer after your child sheepishly informed you that the computer had 'just crashed', there is a reason for that.

> *"Viruses do not just appear magically like mushrooms after a rainstorm. Usually somebody has done something like clicking on a bogus email. This is a huge and growing phenomenon. Criminals want to get malicious code on to your computer and there is good motivation for this – big money."*
> **Marian Merritt, internet security advocate at Norton**

This malicious code, known as 'malware', is the name that has come to cover everything from viruses to spam, spyware, Trojan horses and worms (see Glossary on p165). Malware can wreak costly havoc on a computer.

FACT
- 65% of kids across the globe have been affected by some form of malware.
- 24% of UK children aged eight to 17 have downloaded a virus on to their computer.
- A third of children who know they have downloaded a virus will not tell their parents.[15]

Malware could mean replacing a computer, or you may find yourself faced with a rather large credit card bill or a depleted bank account. The biggest issue when it comes to commercial risk is for your children to understand the importance of privacy.

4

Addiction and other health risks

The health risks associated with the use of the internet, and computers in general, are a subject that many in the industry would prefer to avoid for obvious reasons. But we are gradually gaining more knowledge about the effects of excessive computer use.

Addiction and excessive use

There has been growing concern over the amount of time children spend online, be that playing games or simply surfing the internet.

> *"My 12-year-old brother James has an Xbox and he plays Call of Duty for about four hours a day. He is totally addicted to it. When my parents try to limit the time he plays he just kicks off. Recently he got a letter home from school saying that he had made some racist comments. That really upset my parents."*
> *Catherine, 17*

Increasingly children will use the word 'addicted' to describe their own or others' dependence on the internet or games they play. So is James addicted? Probably not. More likely he is online too much.

> "In the course of my research, I have only come across a handful of people who I would genuinely call addicts. Playing a game excessively does not necessarily mean a child is addicted."
> **Professor Mark Griffiths, International Gaming Research Unit, Nottingham Trent University**

What children think about gaming

- Over half of UK children aged nine to 15 admitted to spending less time with family or friends because of the internet.
- Over a third have tried unsuccessfully to spend less time online.

What makes an addict?

For someone to be addicted they need to be displaying the six core components of addiction. According to Professor Mark Griffiths, a psychologist who has been researching the impact of gaming on people for over two decades, these are:

1. **salience** – when gaming becomes the most important thing in a child's life
2. **mood modification** – this could be described as a 'buzz', a 'high', 'numbing' or an 'escape'
3. **tolerance** – when a child needs more time to achieve the mood change described above
4. **withdrawal symptoms** – an unpleasant feeling or even a physical effect when the child stops playing

5. **conflict** – when the child's friendships, school work, social life and hobbies begin to suffer as a result. They also may experience a sense of personal loss

6. **relapse** – if a child has stopped online gaming for a period and then feels compelled to revert to previous excessive patterns of playing.

The evidence to date is that only a small minority of people become addicted, but sometimes – though not always – it is harder to recognise the signs of addiction in children. Research is also limited, and over time we may get a better idea of the levels of addiction in children.

In the Netherlands and South Korea dedicated treatment clinics have been opened for gaming addiction. China has introduced laws to limit the amount of time adolescents can spend online – though it seems highly unlikely the UK will legislate something like this.

Partial reinforcement effect (PRE)

While our children might not be medically addicted, it is true to say that online gaming can be all-consuming, and look very much like addiction. This is down to something called the partial reinforcement effect, or PRE, says Mark Griffiths.

Gaming developers use techniques to make children want to stay in a game for longer – namely, rewards. The excitement of finding gold, completing a quest, or improving a score are all examples of how PRE works. This may not necessarily lead to addiction but it could result in excessive game playing.

Not all games use PRE – some developers are given a specific brief to ensure that children do not end up in what the industry calls the 'black hole', when they want to keep playing at all costs.

In Chapter 12 we look more closely at how game playing can affect your child, how much time is too much, and how you can make the most of your child's game-playing time.

Radiation from mobile phones

Mobile phones operate using radio frequencies. In very simple terms, then, a mobile phone could be described as a very smart radio. But does radio frequency radiation harm your child? The truth is that the jury is definitely still out on this one.

> FACT 70% of children aged five to 16 have a mobile phone.[16]

What most scientists agree on is this: that the long-term effect of mobile phone use, particularly on children, is a 'known unknown'. In other words, we do not yet know everything there is to know about the harmful effects.

A study into the health effects of electromagnetic radiation, which culminated in the BioInitiative Report in 2007,[17] found that some effects can be shown from existing research, and that further research is needed, but until then the safety standards for exposure need to be more conservative.

In 2009 a study was released by the Interphone Study Group. This is the name given to a series of international case studies assessing whether radio frequency exposure from mobile phones can be linked to cancer risk. The study was partially funded by the mobile industry and the release of the report was delayed for several months. Why?

> "The various stakeholders involved in funding the project were at loggerheads over what spin to put on the results."
> A senior telecoms lawyer who wished to remain anonymous

In time, more information will reveal how big this risk is. In the meantime, if you are worried about radiation and can't stop your child using their mobile altogether, texting is better than talking because the handset is further away from the brain.

Damage to eyesight

Children have more sensitive eyes than adults and extra precautions should be taken to prevent excessive eye strain. Gaming is not the only culprit. General computer use can also prove harmful; the glare from the screen can make it hard for some children to concentrate.

> "I believe that use of video games excessively detracts from the opportunity for children to learn in physical and constructive ways, and that long-term use of video games can affect our ability both to concentrate and to think visually. This can impact on spelling and problem-solving skills and in some cases affect reading comprehension."
> **Keith Holland, an eye specialist**

When it comes to gaming, Holland says 20 to 30 minutes is quite enough for children and they should always play with some sort of back lighting – never in a dark room.

TIP If your child has an eye problem, make sure all teachers are aware of this and ask for printouts which your child may find easier to read.

Stress – the physical and emotional

Children who spend hours in front of a computer screen without taking a break are at risk of repetitive stress injuries. And if too much screen time is making your child's joints hurt, it could be causing them psychological problems.

A Bristol University study showed that ten- and 11-year-olds who spent more than two hours a day at a computer had a 60% higher risk of psychological problems.

But, showing how much technology has become a part of our lives, a study from FOSI revealed that 31% of teens say unplugging from technology made them more stressed.

The negative effects of being online can sometimes be blown out of all proportion, and fixated on by us parents. While we need to be aware of these risks, and approach them sensibly, we must understand this new world we live in. Undoubtedly this involves technology, but is it all bad? Are we destined to become antisocial beings?

Debunking the myths

While the threat of sexual predators to children on the internet is not something to be flippant about, the reality is that the biggest threats our children are likely to face are social and commercial. Of course, we must be aware of and respond to these risks, but we need to be realistic and not exaggerate any negative effects of technology. For one, spending time online does not necessarily mean we will end up as little hobbits, living in a dark room with no friends.

> *"Most people who use social networks are the most socially active in the real world."*
> **Graham Jones, internet psychologist**

In fact one of the original purposes of Facebook was to arrange physical meetings so that groups could collaborate on various assignments. Many people still use Facebook for this purpose today.

So a good first step would be accepting that technology has a powerful influence on our children which, with the right boundaries and terms of use, can be positive. We should also not forget that the internet is a real world occupied by real people – just as we would not send young children out onto the street without a lesson in road safety, the same should be true for the internet. Of course as they get older more freedom is appropriate, providing they have the right skills and understanding to navigate and protect themselves.

Children will take risks and push boundaries – some more than others – and it is our job to make sure they are protected. We should not be controlling but we should be in control.

Myth or fact?

Myth: Paedophiles can be easily identified by their lewd behaviour online

Fact: Paedophiles know to stay under the radar by avoiding using any terminology that could be picked up by filtering software

Myth: The internet is entirely responsible for the early sexualisation of childhood

Fact: Television still has the strongest hold over UK children; 24% of nine- to 16-year-olds saw sexual images on television, more than double the proportion who had seen such images online[18]

Myth: Gaming makes my child lazy and distracts him from doing homework

Fact: Children who are allowed to play age-appropriate games for limited periods are statistically more likely to do homework and take exercise. Gaming can also act as a stress reliever[19]

Myth: Filtering and monitoring software from a trusted brand is enough to keep my child safe on the internet

Fact: Installing decent software is a good first step but there is no substitute for talking to your child about what is and is not appropriate

Myth: Social networking websites like Facebook will make my teenager antisocial

Fact: Studies show that people who are active on social networks are socially active in the real world

Were you surprised by any of the above facts? Did they change the way you view technology? It's easy to fall into the trap of vilifying technology, but what we need to do is understand it, and adapt to it sensibly.

In Part 1 we have covered the various risks your child may face online; now let's move on to what you as a parent can do to protect your child.

Part 2

General safety guidelines

Now you've got a clear handle on the exact risks your child might face, and how likely it is that they may face them, it's time to get practical.

There are a number of steps we can take to help our children become safer online. In this section we will be addressing the general rules you can put in place to help your child, and in Part 3 we go into the specifics.

> "Parents need to think about the internet as another part of everyday life and teach their children to apply the same values, attitudes and moral behaviour online as they do in the real world. This is another dimension to being a modern parent and equates to teaching them sex education, not to get into cars with strangers and to look both ways when they cross the road."
> **John Carr, adviser to the UK Government and United Nations on child online safety**

Some of the advice in this section may seem like common sense and some of you will have heard it before, but there may be some surprises too.

6

Communicating
with your child

Of all the pieces of advice included in this book, it is clear that one thing is more important than the others: communication. Every expert interviewed agreed that talking – and, even more importantly, listening – to our children about their online experience is our most powerful tool. When it comes to communicating the message of online safety, parents have a central role to play. It may not always seem so but children do actually take in what their parents are saying.

It's clear that communication is vital – but what and how do we communicate? One of the challenges parents face is that communication is very personal. Just as there are many different ways to parent, there are just as many ways to communicate to different types of children.

> *"There is no right or wrong way to do things and we certainly do not have a template for parents to follow. What we want is for parents to engage with their children so they are able to make good decisions whenever they go online, especially because things are going increasingly mobile."*
> **Will Gardner, chief executive, Childnet International**

One major batch of research shows that UK parents are not doing too badly in positively mediating their children's internet use, and communication seems to play a central role in this.

FACT
- Over 74% of parents talk to their children about what they do online.
- 90% are confident they can help their child if they have a bad experience.[20]

So is that a good indication of how parents feel? Other evidence suggests that while we might try to communicate, the quality of what we are communicating may be a problem – many of us still feel our children know more than we do. That is not a good place to be if we want to parent confidently.

FACT
- Nearly half of us with children aged five to 15 feel we know less than our children about using the internet.
- 70% of parents of 12- to 15-year-olds think their children know more than them.[21]

Having spoken to many parents in the course of researching this book, what seems certain is that most want to know more and some certainly need to know more.

It seems, however, that many of us are now less worried than we used to be about how our children use the internet. Even though our children are online at a much younger age we are now less likely to set parental controls (37% in 2010 versus 43% in 2009).[22] Is this because we trust our children or feel we are supervising them adequately, or are we simply burying our heads in the sand?

Is communication enough?

Claire, mum to Max (9) and Lily (7), works in the criminal justice system and spends much of her time witnessing the darker side of human nature. "I took a decision when my children were quite young to tell them about child abuse in language they could understand otherwise I would never have wanted to let them out of my sight," she says.

Claire has spoken to her children about internet safety and they know not to give out personal information or meet anybody they have met online. It is clear they have an open relationship and the children know they can talk to their mum if they encounter something strange online. Once Lily came across a swear word on a game and so they agreed that this was not suitable. The computers are in the family room and the children mainly play games like Moshi Monsters and Club Penguin. So far Claire has not invested in any filtering or monitoring software but she knows she should.

It seems as if Claire's doing an OK job, but probe a little deeper and it soon becomes clear that the children do indeed know more than their mum. At first Claire seems quite confident that Club Penguin only uses pre-scripted chat but Max is quick to correct her: "Oh no, Mum – you can chat freely. You just have to change the settings."

Does Max go online on his Xbox? "Oh no," says Claire, "you can't go online. He just plays innocent football games like Fifa 11." Max, it would appear, knows better: "Yes you can go online on the Xbox."

"But you don't do you?" says his mum. His response: "Well, no – it is too slow."

This story probably sums up where we are as parents. We are far from as ignorant as many professionals in the world of e-safety would have us believe, but we are not there yet.

Are Max and Lily going to get in trouble online? Probably not. Claire may not fully understand what they are up to but they have an open and trusting relationship. As a busy working mum, Claire is also pragmatic, arguing that just as she could not possibly read everything her children read, so she simply cannot be there all the time when they are online. She is absolutely right – we cannot monitor everything our children do.

> TIP Take an interest in what your children are doing online. Set some time aside – perhaps once a month – to ask them to show you round their virtual worlds. Keep the lines of communication open and remember to listen too.

How to communicate

In the past decade how we communicate has changed and our children are leading the way on many fronts. We cannot stop humans from communicating but we can and should talk to our children about *how* to communicate. If you try to control *what* they say, they will do it behind your back; but it is important to explain that there are boundaries for responsible behaviour.

> *"Young people benefit from being shown the boundaries of free expression and it should be made explicitly clear to them that those boundaries are not unfettered but have reasonable limits."*
> **Dr Shane Gallagher, educational and child psychologist**

One way of getting across the implications of their online activity is to open a discussion about how their online behaviour could be viewed in the real world. Talk to them matter-of-factly and honestly and listen to what they have to say. Ask the following questions.

- Would they want grandma to see a photograph or video clip of them after indulging in too much cider?
- Would they tell the person loitering on a street corner where they lived?

- Would they cross a road without looking both ways?
- Would they call a friend a 'whore' or 'slag' to their face?
- How might they feel if the tables were turned and they were on the receiving end of cruel or unkind remarks?

> TIP It is essential that this conversation is not a one-time occurrence but is an ongoing discussion, because children forget. One in ten eight- to 15-year-olds say they forget about the safety rules when using the internet.[23]

What to communicate

In the age of social media, and especially mobile social media, we need to teach our children and teenagers to apply common sense at all times. They need to keep their wits about them, thinking before they sign into something or post too much information about others or themselves.

By sticking to a few simple rules which encourage responsible conduct, most risks can be avoided. This advice applies across every single online activity your child may be involved in – from social networking to instant messaging or gaming – and is particularly important in the mobile world.

Online safety essentials

- Keep personal information private – never give out your email address, physical address or phone number to a person you do not trust completely.
- Never share passwords, not even with close friends.
- Change passwords regularly.
- Use different passwords for every service you access and store these in a safe place.

- Be aware that not everybody you meet online is who they say they are. Some people pretend to be older or younger than they are. Some may falsely claim to be celebrities.

  > *"My eight-year-old niece is a big fan of Justin Bieber.*
  > *She googled 'Justin Bieber's Moshi Monster profile' and*
  > *sent a message to that person. When I asked her how*
  > *she knew for sure it was Justin Bieber it was obvious that*
  > *this had not even crossed her mind."*
  > **Mary, 39**

- Remember to log off after using a device.
- Do not post provocative images of yourself on the internet and check with others before posting a photograph of somebody else – if grandma would not want to read it or see it, it is probably best kept private.
- Don't use illegal file-sharing sites to download music or films illegally – it is a criminal offence.
- Never open an attachment, email or link unless you are sure where it came from.
- Financial information (credit card details, PayPal and so on) should only be used with parents' permission first (see p20). Parents should sign up to a verification system like MasterCard's SecureCode or Verified by Visa with a password only they are aware of, to add another level of secure verification.
- Think before you post and be kind to others online – the golden rule is that you should not post anything you would not feel comfortable saying to somebody in person or that you would not want to receive yourself.
- Think very, very carefully before accepting friend requests from strangers or meeting an online contact in real life.

Password privacy – a hard lesson

Kim, 54, is a mum of five. Maggie, her youngest, is ten years old and has learnt the hard way about the importance of keeping her password safe. "When the email came from Build-A-Bear saying that Maggie had been abusive to other users and was being permanently barred from using the site, I was shocked," says Kim. Refusing to believe that her child was capable of this, she emailed Build-A-Bear to request an investigation. They responded with a sentence-by-sentence conversation that was sent to other 'bears' supposedly by her daughter.

Five days earlier Maggie's mobile phone had been stolen at school and the thief had sent several texts to Kim. "It was uncanny as the word 'monkey' was used a few times in these messages," says Kim.

When Build-A-Bear supplied Kim with the IP address of the user who had sent the messages she was not surprised to find that it was different to her own. It also turns out that messages were sent between 10.30 and noon when my daughter was at school. As it turns out, Maggie had given her password for Build-A-Bear to her friend who had also 'borrowed' the mobile phone as a joke.

Double standards?

Most parents will make it clear to their child that it is dangerous to meet an online contact in the real world. But is this realistic given that increasingly the web is becoming a place to meet and connect with like-minded people?

> "I'm a single mum and have recently started using websites like the Guardian's Soulmates and Match.com to meet people. So when I tell my kids they should never meet anybody they have met online it feels a bit hypocritical."
> **Sasha, 43**

She has a point. Once again a bit of common sense will not go awry. Obviously we would not want our very young children to be meeting up with people they have met online. But teenagers are increasingly using the internet to connect with people they may not have met before, with around 39% of nine- to 16-year-olds having looked for new friends online.[24]

> *"I'm not allowed on Facebook but I have an account anyway.*
> *My parents would absolutely die if they knew I had met up*
> *with a stranger. But I told my friends I was going to and went*
> *ahead and met him. It turns out he is a really nice person."*
> **Nadirah, 16**

Children who feel unable to talk to their parents are more likely to take risks. The moral of this story is: keep those lines of communication open and chances are you will have a much better idea of what is going on in their lives. That can only be a good thing when they reach those tricky teenage years.

TIP Tell your teenager that if they absolutely must meet an online contact in the real world, they should meet in a public place, take somebody with them the first time and let you know where they are going.

Does communication work?

The good news is that the messages children are receiving at school, or from their parents, about keeping personal information private seem to be getting through.

FACT Children aged 12 to 15 are much less willing to give out contact details (22%), their mobile number (8%) or home address details (6%) than they were a few years ago.[25]

The not-so-good news is that many children are still posting photographs of themselves out with friends (58%), or information about what they are doing (51%) and how they are feeling (46%).[26] This is not necessarily a problem, providing they are sensible about what they post. Giving too much information about their whereabouts is not a good idea. This is especially true in the age of smart mobile phones that are embedded with geolocation technology (see p145), where online activity can take place at any time or in any place, making a child's whereabouts easily known to anybody. 'Sharing' on Facebook could also lead to problems.

> "My son went away on a school trip and we had this exchange online where he was saying how much he hated it and how homesick he was. He was teased terribly afterwards."
> Jennifer, mum to Justin (15)

Advice from our children

Who better to ask about what communication methods work best than children themselves? Here are some of the things they had to say.

- Listen to what we have to say.
- Get to know what we are doing online – some of it is good fun and we even learn a few things on the way.
- Encourage our creativity online.
- Do not overreact when we do something daft.
- Do not be too strict – we'll find a way around it and that might cause you embarrassment.

Minimising your digital footprint

Now that we have covered the basics, we need to take this a step further. Talking to our children about what to post and how to post it is really important – so important that not doing so could place them at unnecessary risk. This does not mean that they should stop doing the things they love, but they should be aware that minimising their 'digital footprint' is something they will not live to regret.

Think of a digital footprint as the trail your child leaves as they move between different virtual worlds. Each internet-enabled device has something called an IP address, which is a bit like a telephone number and identifies where information is being sent from. Without it computers cannot communicate with each other.

Tips for minimising a digital footprint

1. When posting information on social networks, do this after an event rather than before.

2. Never name people when you are posting in real time from a mobile: instead, use a nickname for your friends or relatives. Nobody needs to know who you are with. In the same vein, do not state where you are posting from.

3. Do not announce to the world that your family is going on holiday as you are heading for the motorway.

4. Assume that the entire world can see everything you post to the internet – would you want your potential future employers to know everything about you and your friends – and what you get up to?

5. Only use trusted wireless networks.

The problem of peer pressure

Children have always faced peer pressure in some form or other, and the desire to fit in and be liked is very much a part of this. But in a consumer-driven world the pressure on children to have the latest gadget, be playing the latest game or participating in 'cool' social networks like Facebook (even if they are under age) is enormous.

The hype that surrounds the release of any new device or console sends pulses racing and turns playgrounds across the country into a frenzy of excitement.

*"Some of the boys at my school stay up all night when a
new game is about to be released. They talk about nothing
else and then they play all night."*
Mark, 15

The resulting peer pressure can become a problem for parents – at
least for our bank balances. It's not easy for children and it's also not
easy for parents.

*"Our ten-year-old daughter really wants a Facebook
account because all her close friends are on it. We have said
no but it is really hard sticking to our guns as she seems to
feel really left out in conversations."*
Graham, dad to Alice (10)

*"My five-year-old son was desperate to get a DS because
most of his friends had one. Eventually we gave in and
now we spend most of the time threatening to take it away
from him."*
Karen, mum to Daniel (5) and Abigail (3)

If this is something you are familiar with, start a discussion about
peer pressure with your child: talk to them about what peer pressure
is and how they might feel.

- Share your own experiences of dealing with it, if you have any.
- Explain that peer pressure is not always bad and can be used
  positively – like a group getting together to stop the bullying of
  another child.
- Get to know your child's friends and their parents.
- Be the scapegoat – let your child blame you if they are trying to
  extricate themselves from a tricky scenario.

Above all the advice given in this chapter, there's one thing you
must remember, and it's simple: keep talking and listening to your
child.

7

Setting rules, establishing boundaries

There can be no disputing that all children benefit from having boundaries that are age-appropriate. Like all forms of parenting, the level of involvement for younger children is much higher than it would be for a teenager. So, for example, just as most of us would not let our six-year-old go to the park alone, by the time they are teenagers this would be appropriate. It is essential for parents to recognise that the internet is a virtual world inhabited by real people. Many children are not only meeting up with their real-world friends online but may also be making new contacts.

> *"Just as you would want to know your children's friend in the real world, it is important to get to know their online friends too."*
> **Marian Merritt, internet security advocate at Norton**

Of course rules will vary from family to family and will very much depend upon the age and nature of the child. Indeed, more often than not we parents are the best judge of how much rein we can give our children. But if you can remember what it was like to be a teenager, you will probably have some recollection of bending the truth to avoid getting into trouble. So while establishing trust between ourselves and our children is very important, the reality is that most children will push boundaries.

Being informed is essential – if our children think they know more than us, they are likely to push these boundaries even further. You cannot set rules if you do not know what they are for.

> *"Parents of children aged six to 11 absolutely have to be in control of their child's online life. We have been saying this for 18 years and many are still not doing it."*
> **Rebecca Newton, chief community and safety officer at Mind Candy, the company behind Moshi Monsters**

At the most basic level parents should:

- understand the risks
- when it comes to younger children (under 12s), make sure you are there to help them set up their online accounts – and then manage those too!
- know how to check online browsing histories and cookies in the temporary internet folder. However, be aware that histories can very easily be deleted and if your child has something to hide, chances are they will have done that (see p126)
- have age-appropriate parental controls installed on their computer
- be aware of what games and services your children are using – are they age-appropriate?
- know how to set passwords in a games console
- understand what a bogus website looks like, what spam is and so on
- know how to save and print the screen of a web page
- keep communicating with your child.

Making rules together

While parents need to be in control, the best way to establish effective rules is to agree them, and the consequences of breaking them, together. Of course it is essential that you have some clear, informed ideas before this discussion begins. For younger children the rules will be stricter and there will be less room for debate. Here are some ideas that have worked for parents interviewed for this book.

- Inform your children that – assuming you have installed some parental control software – you will receive activity reports on their internet usage. If you have agreed the rules with them it will be much easier to enforce these rules.
- Tell them while it is very easy to delete histories, they should also know that nothing can ever be permanently deleted.
- Homework should be done before any online leisure activity – chatting, gaming, social networking – starts.
- If your child has their own laptop and is allowed to use it in their bedroom, agree that homework is done in a family space.
- Agree the amount of leisure time your child will spend online each day. Get them to think through what they think is enough and why. Stick to this.
- Discuss what content is suitable (see the section on filtering and monitoring on p58).
- Agree a time for devices to be switched off. Children (and indeed adults) need to wind down before sleeping and too much screen time late at night can affect sleep patterns.

Should the computer be in the family room?

Ask any internet safety expert and the answer to this question is a resounding yes. But the arrival of internet-enabled mobile phones, and tablet devices like the iPad, has complicated matters somewhat.

"When you start to think about children accessing the internet from a mobile phone or an iPad, the widely given advice that your children should only access the internet in the family room at home starts to look distinctly dated."
William Webb, futurologist and author of Wireless
Communications: The future

As the cost of internet use comes down and devices become cheaper, more children are likely to have access in their bedrooms. Even today, the latest figures shed some light on just how connected our children are.

FACT Of UK children aged five to 16:
* 95% have a computer or laptop at home
* 85% use the internet
* 45% have their own laptop
* 46% have internet access in their room
* 65% go online every day or most days.[27]

Regardless of these statistics, for children under 12, having the computer in the family room is still a good idea. When they get a bit older more flexibility can be introduced but parents must continue to show an interest in what their children are doing.

How much is too much time online?

This is a very tough call. 'Screen time is screen time' is the mantra of many experts (in other words, texting, browsing, television etc. should all be counted). One study by the University of Bristol[28] assessed over a thousand children aged around ten to 11 and found that children who spend longer than two hours a day in front of a screen are more likely to suffer psychological difficulties, even if they had taken adequate exercise. There have been other reports[29] which suggest that too much screen time raises the risk of heart disease. But how scientific are these studies? How much screen time is too much and are some kinds of screen time better than others?

Two hours a day seems somewhat unrealistic against the backdrop of these global statistics.

- In 2004 young people spent 6.5 hours with media, or 8.5 hours a day if you count multitasking.
- In 2011 the figure is 7.5 hours a day, seven days a week – or 10.75 hours a day if you count multitasking.[30]

The messages are confusing, and the statistics don't seem possible. On the one hand, child development and health professionals are telling us to limit the time our children spend in front of screens. But on the other hand we have our schools sending home usernames and passwords for children as young as five to access the 'managed learning environments' (MLEs) which are being rolled out by most local authorities in the UK (see p69).

This leaves us wondering how much screen time is okay. There is certainly one emerging view that children who do not spend enough time doing positive things online will find themselves on the wrong side of the digital divide (see Chapter 18). So perhaps it's not how much time they are online, but what they are doing during that time that really matters.

> "Sometimes what we want for our children is what we perceive to be balance, but often we don't ask our children enough what it is that they want or need."
> **Graham Jones, internet psychologist**

Instead Jones says we should be asking ourselves these questions: is my child suffering as a result of what they are doing? Are we stimulating their creativity to ensure that they get maximum benefit from the online world? It may be, for example, that your child is spending all the time possible online because they are passionate about something.

> *"Charlie will obsessively make mini-films and then spend days editing. He is in front of a screen a lot and I am okay with that as long as he is being creative."*
> **Miranda, mum to Charlie (9) and Georgia (8)**

Managing screen time

Ultimately children learn by example. So if you are constantly in front of a screen do not expect them to behave differently. Every so often unplug from everything.

Here, other parents share their ideas for limiting screen time.

> *"During the holidays, our rule is no screens between 10am and 6pm. That forces me to get out and about with the children during the day."*
> **Kate, mum to Harry (11) and Jessica (10)**

> *"Once a month we have a day of no screens. The children always moan about it beforehand but it is always really good to remind ourselves what life was like before the internet. I'm not sure we could do it for longer though."*
> **Jack, dad to Daniel (13) and Emily (8)**

> *"I encourage the children to plan their screen time. They decide what they want to watch on telly and what games they want to play online. We then discuss whether this is reasonable or not. That way they get to moderate their own screen time and it minimises conflict when rules are broken."*
> **Arati, mum to Aatifa (12) and Maha (9)**

"I encourage my son to use websites that mirror his real-world interests – he is obsessed with football. My thinking is that if he is playing sports-based games or looking at these websites he will eventually want to go out and kick a ball around."
Nick, dad to Evan (13)

What to do if they break the rules

Until recently, a common approach was to ban children from using technology for a set period if they broke the rules set by parents. However, increasingly experts recognise that this does not work and may in fact result in children being less likely to tell their parents if they encounter something that bothers them.

The bottom line here is that children do not want to lose access to their online world and once the lines of communication between you and your child are closed, these are difficult to re-open.

"We recently asked our older children if they would tell somebody if they encountered something that bothered them online and it was surprising – and also worrying – how many of them said no because they didn't want to lose the privilege."
Linda, ICT co-ordinator at a London primary school

Once again it comes down to common sense. If a child's obsession with a game is affecting your family life then strong action like banning the activity may be the only solution. If a child is a cyber-bully this may also be an effective response (more on this on p79).

Top tips from parents for establishing boundaries and rules

"When my kids break the rules the punishment is something that makes my life easier – like cleaning the toilets for the month, or doing the monthly shop."
Davina, mum to Harriet (15), Damian (10) and Milly (5)

"Our computer is in our family room and the boys play games in here too. That way at least we get to see our teenagers even if they are in front of screens. We can also monitor if homework is being done."
John, dad to Callum (15) and Tim (13)

"Homework and music practice before anything else. Simple."
Gill, mum to Joseph (12) and Anna (10)

"Our children can only use the internet during the week if it relates to homework which they do in a public space. On the weekends they can do their own thing but we limit that to two or three hours a day."
Matthew, dad to Anna (14) and Jack (12)

"No mobile phones or any devices in the bedroom after 9pm. Children need to wind down from screens before they sleep."
Fleur, mum to Sophie (16) and Pierre (12)

"I'm a computer programmer so told my teenage daughter I could see everything she was doing online if I wanted to. She believed me and it worked."
May, mum to Elena (16), Andrew (7) and Lyle (5)

Privacy – how much should you respect theirs?

We have talked about teaching your child not to give out too much personal information online to protect their privacy; but how much should we invade theirs? Monitoring is a common tactic of UK parents – more than half of us do it.[31] By monitoring we mean actively checking what websites your child is visiting, checking up on their social networking profiles or scrolling through their histories. Unsurprisingly, this can cause arguments and undermine trust.

Finding the right balance between keeping our children safe and respecting their privacy is a tough call. Monitoring may be one strategy but it is less effective than positive support, offering appropriate safety guidance and setting clear rules.

> **TIP** Unless you have very real concerns, do not read your teenager's email or steal their password to access an account. If you do you will almost certainly destroy their trust in you and the all-important ability to communicate with them may be lost forever.

Technical solutions
Parental control

We've established that communication is the most powerful tool we have as parents, and setting rules and boundaries is as important as ever. But what else can you do?

If we are going to give our children a degree of freedom based on trust, and not monitor their actions rigidly, we need to make sure there are boundaries in place to stop them accessing the whole of the web in one click. This is where technical solutions can help.

> **FACT** Only 46% of UK parents have invested in parental control tools to filter or block websites – that's better than our European counterparts (28%) but still means over half of parents don't have the tools in place.[32]

One thing is certain: if you have no parental controls, chances are that sooner rather than later your child will be exposed to inappropriate content.

"My eldest is six and has started going online because he has been given login details for his school's managed learning environment. Recently he had some friends to play and they were searching for games. They put some innocent word into a search engine and ended up on a porn site. I wasn't expecting this so soon but I had to tell their parents. It was very embarrassing."
Sue, mum to Michael (6), Jane (4) and Daniel (8 months)

What you need from safety software

The ideal software package allows parents to:

1. create different profiles or accounts for different users in the home

2. customise web content so that certain websites are filtered or shown according to specific defined criteria. So, for example, the parent would be able to block certain topics or keywords such as 'porn' or 'violence'. The parent could also create a list of desired websites or keywords

3. blacklist or whitelist certain websites (see box on p59)

4. block or filter usage of certain applications. So, for example, the tool would prevent children from watching videos using streaming software or using instant messenger services like Skype or Windows Live Messenger

5. monitor the use of various applications and receive a report of the child's activity. This could include what websites they have visited, for how long, and who they have chatted to using an instant messenger service

6. set a time limit for use and notify the parent when that has been exceeded.

Blacklists versus whitelists

Blacklisting blocks *specific* websites that are defined in a list by the parent; all other websites are allowed. When it comes to instant messaging or online calls, a blacklist could be created to block SMS messages or calls that match the entries in the list. All other messages or calls would be allowed. (The settings of some mobile phones allow you to create specific user lists too.)

Whitelisting blocks *all* internet sites *apart* from the websites you have defined in a list. When it comes to SMS messages or calls, only numbers matching those in the whitelist would be allowed. All other messages or calls would be blocked.

Read more on p106 about how websites use these lists.

TIP When a site is blocked by parental controls, there is sometimes the option for your child to 'request access'. You will then be informed that they want to access this site, and can allow access if you feel it's appropriate. Encouraging them to ask you makes them less likely to try to get around your parental controls.

What to consider when investing in parental control software for any device

1. What kind of content can be filtered using this software?

Most parents will think of adult content when purchasing a safety solution and this is the content that is filtered best. But there are other types of harmful content (violence, racism, self-harm, eating disorders and gambling) which are very difficult to filter.

2. What sites or services exactly can the software filter?

This is important as your child will most likely be using a whole range of applications so it is worth understanding what the software covers. For example, does it protect your child when they are using the internet, email, Skype, Windows Live Messenger, chat rooms or peer-to-peer file-sharing websites? If you are worried about your child on Windows Live Messenger, be aware that at the time of going to press only four tools allowed the possibility to filter contacts.

3. How does the software filter emails, social networks like Facebook or instant messaging services like Windows Live Messenger or Skype?

For parents of under-13s it is important to know that you can block your child from accessing Facebook or other age-restricted sites. For older children you may wish to block the sites during homework time.

4. How efficient is the software and what is the support service for less tech-savvy parents?

Usability is very important and quite often it is difficult to understand what exactly will be filtered and it is even less easy to install and set up. Companies should be able to give you a clear picture of how effective their software is and offer appropriate support.

5. Are the software updates done in real time?

If you are a parent who is likely to forget to update the software then this might be useful.

6. Does the tool allow the parent to create and manage different profiles for different users?

This is important as it will allow you to set the parameters depending on the age group and will also allow you to limit how much time your child spends online.

7. Does the software provide a report of a user's web activity?

Around 20% of tools tested during one study did not provide a basic report of activity.

8. Does the software monitor the activity or the device that a child is using?

Some software will monitor activity across devices, which is useful when you consider that many children now use their mobile phone to go online.

9. Is the child involved in setting the boundaries?

This is a useful way to open a discussion about keeping safe online.

10. How easily can software be bypassed or disabled?

For parents of children who are more tech-savvy than they are, this is important to know. See p63 for more on undoing parental controls.

Do they work?

Now we know what you ideally want from software, where do you get it? And does it actually work?

When researching safety software you will face a myriad of choices, and there is a wide range of products to choose from. The bad news is that so far the parental control tools currently on the market are not proving to be very effective!

The European Commission's Safer Internet Programme (SIP) is involved in an ongoing independent study into the effectiveness of parental control software[33] for personal computers, mobile devices and gaming consoles. These are currently the three main ways children access the internet. The software available was scored out of four points according to:

- **functionality** – could the software block content according to different categories, did it offer different profiles for different users, was it possible to whitelist or blacklist specific websites and did it provide web activity reports and so on?
- **effectiveness** – once the parents had set the functions, how effective were these? In other words, did it actually filter the content from the categories set by parents? One of the big problems with software is that while it may filter harmful content, at the same time it may stop the user looking at content which is perfectly safe, thus defeating the object
- **usability** – how easy was it to configure and install?
- **security** – how easily could a child bypass the filters?

Each parent will have different requirements. For example, for less tech-savvy parents, usability will be very important. However, for parents with very technology-literate children (and there are plenty of those), security that prevents a child bypassing filters will be even more relevant.

> *"You would be absolutely amazed by just how many children know how to bypass supposedly secure systems to access the content they want."*
> **Christopher Boyd, senior threat researcher, GFI Software**

The most important point above is of course the effectiveness of the software. But it is on this score that many products fare worst. Without exception, all the tools tested by SIP at the time of going to press had low effectiveness, especially for web 2.0 content (blogs and social networks). When it came to effectiveness, *all* the tools failed to block more than 20% of harmful content.

> *"It is difficult to define what should be satisfactory effectiveness, but certainly if tools are less than 50% effective they are not good enough and parents should be aware of this."*
> **Jérôme Valette, lead computer scientist on SIP study**

In spite of the limitations, we should not write off technical solutions completely. Many will certainly filter explicit keywords, for example, and have the ability to block big offending websites with obvious harmful content in their title. Most also allow parents to create and manage different profiles and can limit the amount of time a user is online. However, technical tools remain just one part of the solution and ongoing education of and communication with our children is still essential.

> **TIP** The SIP study is ongoing and will be updated every six months until the end of 2012. At all stages of the process the information will be made public. For detailed results of the study and to search for software that best suits your needs, go to www.yprt.eu/sip.

Undoing parental controls

You'll probably have heard of instances where our clever children have managed to bypass the parental controls we have set and changed them to suit their needs.

Firstly, it's absolutely vital that you password-protect your parental controls and software settings. It sounds obvious, but an additional thing to be aware of is what your password actually is: use one unknown to your children – and one that they can't easily work out! Avoid using dates of birthdays, phone numbers or the same password as any other account you might have. This needs to be un-crackable!

Secondly, many children turn to YouTube to watch videos that show how to undo the parental controls. The videos tell you how to go into the computer's set-up and alter the settings or even restore factory settings.

"My parents put the parental controls on my Xbox so I couldn't chat to other people. So I went on YouTube and found out how to undo them."
Sam, 12

Our kids are smart and can use technology against us. This may be a continuing problem, as teenagers grow ever more IT-skilled. It's not helped by the fact that the software available cannot be relied upon fully. To echo the advice given in Chapter 6, the best way around this is to stop your teen *wanting* to bypass your controls – by explaining why they're there, and discussing what sites they would like access to and why.

(You might also want to know that while Sam was typing 'how to undo...' into YouTube's search engine he found the first line of predictive text was 'how to undo her pants'. See Chapter 14 for more information on filtering content on YouTube.)

> **TIP** One way children get around blocked content is to get their friends to email it to them. This is where your software should kick in and block any inappropriate content, so make sure you know if your software is capable of this.

The mobile picture – smartphones, tablets and consoles

While there might be a lot of choice when it comes to your computer, you'll find that when it comes to mobile devices – like smartphones, tablets and consoles – the solutions for filtering and monitoring present an even bleaker picture. There may be many tools for mobile phones to turn off web browsing, but at the time of going to press only a few were able to actually filter web content effectively.

Consoles tend to have embedded parental control tools but most are focused on the activities that happen within games, such as chatting or purchasing in-game currency. Again, none of the tools tested by SIP was able to filter web pages according to content.

The tablet market is growing steadily, and at the time of going to press parental control products for Apple's iPad were the same as those for the iPhone. When it comes to Google's Android tablets there were virtually no solutions, and they could not use the software available for personal computers.

> TIP In Part 3 we'll look at possible solutions for these devices. See p140 for more on smartphones, and p150 for more on tablets.

Software that spies – is it a good idea?

There are many 'big brother'-type products, such as SpectorPro, IamBigBrother and SniperSpy, which you can use to spy on your child while they are online without their knowledge. But is this a good idea? Once again this comes down to your parenting style. If you choose this road, be warned that if your child finds out it may be very difficult to rebuild a relationship based on trust.

It is widely agreed that talking to your children about internet safety is far more effective.

> *"When you are looking for a technical solution you should definitely be looking for one that involves your children in the process by encouraging them to talk about internet safety. It should give your kids a voice in setting the rules because then they will be much more likely to follow them."*
> **Marian Merritt, internet security advocate at Norton**

Network-level security

One thing is certain. This is a fast-moving environment and there are new developments constantly. Parents need to remain on top of these as they happen because before long there may soon be a solution that really does what it says on the box.

While there will never be a product that can replace parental responsibility entirely, companies keen to stand out in a competitive environment are working hard to improve solutions.

Network-level security is one way to do this. This differs from traditional software solutions in that it is configured when you install your home internet connection and works on any device that is connected to the home network, including laptops, personal computers, smartphones and games consoles.

> *"Many children now use their mobile to go online so the overall effectiveness of device-based controls is decreasing. In other words the product needs to monitor the activity rather than the device."*
> **Rik Ferguson, director of security, research and communication, EMEA Trend Micro**

TIP Check with your internet service provider what solutions they have on offer. In May 2011 TalkTalk launched the first network-level security solution in the UK, and others are bound to follow suit. HomeSafe blocks inappropriate websites and content from all devices using the home network, and also protects you against malware and viruses.

Products that monitor activity across all the devices children use – from laptops to mobile phones, tablets and games consoles – which are updated in real time, and which allow parents to access reports from any internet-connected device, will become increasingly common. This is the way internet safety is progressing, and it makes sense with the myriad of devices we can now access the internet on.

However, even network-level security is not perfect and will not stop your child accessing the internet via a 3G mobile network, separate to your home network. Communication with your child is still the most effective tool.

Why using a trusted network matters

According to Mike Hawkes, chairman of the Mobile Data Association, one of the big problems right now is that there is no cross-network security in the mobile world. While the mobile networks do provide parental controls, nothing prevents a child from switching to a nearby wifi network that offers none of these protection mechanisms.

Here is an example of how this might impact commercially on your child. A 15-year-old girl is sitting in a coffee shop, waiting for a friend to arrive. She checks what wifi networks are available and sees that there is one called coffeeshop1. Better still, it is free. As it turns out, this is an insecure network and a few seconds later she receives a message asking her to download an application (or simply click on a link) to claim a free hot chocolate. Like you, she does not read the small print. Guess what? It turns out this is a malicious virus and before long your bank details, which you gave her to buy a song on iTunes, have been compromised. Worse still, this handset can then compromise all her friends' compatible mobile devices as soon as they come into range.

E-safety policies
in schools
What you need to know

Our children spend a good deal of their lives at school and using the internet from primary school level is increasingly common. So why is it important for parents to understand what their children are being taught in school?

In order to stay safe online, our children must become 'digitally literate'. Digital, or media, literacy is the ability to use, understand and create media and communications. While our older children are doing okay on this front, when it comes to younger children there are significant gaps in their safety skills. Around a third of 11- and 12-year-olds cannot bookmark a site and even more cannot block unwanted messages.[34]

What and how your child is taught

Besides parents, schools will play a central role in what our children are taught. Parents should take an active interest in how information technology is being taught in school and establish exactly what children are learning. Ask your child's school these questions.

- How is IT taught in the school: is it included across the curriculum, is it taught as a separate subject, or both?
- What training is available to teachers to ensure they are keeping pace with technological advances?
- Given how easy it is to plagiarise content today, are children being taught how to research rather than copy? How is this done?
- Does the school run courses for parents so they are aware of how their children can maximise the use of virtual or managed learning environments (see below)?
- Are children taught how to recognise a dodgy website or recognise what spam is?
- What resources do teachers use for teaching purposes?
- All schools must teach internet safety, but how is it taught and does it include parental education? If so, what awareness initiatives are they making use of? For example, do they run parental education evenings or have any material available for parents?

> TIP Many schools are embracing technology and adopting managed learning environments (MLEs) or virtual learning environments (VLEs). Children as young as five will be using computers at school and given passwords to access networks from home. This means our children will be going online at a much younger age – so it's even more important that you're aware of your school's e-safety policy.

When Sparklebox lost its sparkle...

Sparklebox was a much-loved teacher resource and one of the UK's biggest education websites until the police uncovered that it was being run by a convicted paedophile. The site, which allowed teachers to create fantastic classroom resources, was run by 28-year-old Daniel Kinge, who launched the site under a new name after he was jailed for nine months back in 2005 for downloading pornographic images of children. At the time he was working at a Warwickshire school. In January 2011 he was jailed for a year after admitting making more than 400 indecent photographs of children. Many local authorities moved to ban schools from using the site.[35] Some teachers have argued that there is no problem with the resources *per se*, while others believe continuing to use the site is tacitly supporting the activity of a child abuser.

E-safety policies

Aside from establishing how IT is being taught, parents should also understand the school's e-safety policy. All schools must teach internet safety but it is really important to fully understand what safety procedures a school has in place for internet use.

Questions to ask of your school's internet and e-safety policy

* Does the school have an acceptable use policy (AUP)? An AUP is a document signed by parents, students, guardians or carers which details how the internet can be used. Not every school has the same policy but most will cover the Computer Misuse Act of 1990. As parents we should be looking for a policy that ensures that the systems our children are using are safe systems and that safe practice is encouraged.

- What filtering and monitoring systems do they use? In many schools this will be managed by the local authority but this is not always the case as quite often these systems are expensive so some schools choose their own.
- Are there clear reporting procedures? For example, is there a named e-safety member of staff for the child or parent to contact in the event of an issue arising? Or do several staff members have e-safety responsibility?
- Does the school distinguish between traditional bullying and cyber-bullying and how active is it in raising awareness about the issue? Educating children in small groups, during circle time for example, and addressing the issue in school assemblies are things to look out for.
- Are there clear sanctions when abuse happens? Are these sanctions punitive or restorative? There is a growing view among educational psychologists that children are much more likely to make changes to their behaviour when people in positions of authority do things with them rather than to them.

> *"I've seen this approach work incredibly well in some schools but it has to be driven from the top. In other words senior leaders in the school have to buy into it."*
> **Teresa Bliss, educational psychologist**

- Are there clear, specific and enforceable rules for the use of mobiles and hand-held consoles in school? Are those rules actually based on mutual respect and trust or do they dictate terms? Are children involved in shaping the rules – is there, for example, a school council where the children can challenge rules that might appear too draconian?
- Is the policy framed in terms the child can understand and does it encourage and promote positive behaviour?
- At what age does e-safety education begin? E-safety education should begin as soon as children begin using computers. In some UK schools children as young as three are accessing virtual learning environments in school.

"We believe that educating young people in how to be safe when online should begin when they first start using the internet."
Helen King, head of education, CEOP

Schools should be able to demonstrate that they have taken reasonable steps to ensure that your child is safe online. If your school's e-safety policy is not up to scratch you should make an appointment to see the head teacher and begin to lobby for improvements. Get other parents involved; some schools run parents' forums and this may be the place to talk about this.

10

Cyber-bullying

Nobody wants to see their child experience emotional distress. In Part 1 (p15) we touched on cyber-bullying as one of the risks our children face online. Cyber-bullying now happens across many devices and is a growing problem, even in primary schools. In this chapter we delve deeper into the forms it can take and offer some clear advice.

To recap, cyber-bullying is the deliberate, repeated and intentional victimisation of a person, who cannot easily defend themselves, by using an electronic medium.

Some acts of cyber-bullying are easy to recognise but it is not always straightforward. For example, several malicious messages sent by text or to the web are clearly cyber-bullying. But it could be less obvious, such as hacking into somebody's account and changing their profile or posting embarrassing personal information about another person. While this may be done as a joke, because of the impersonal nature of the internet, facial expression and tone are absent and this action could prove to be devastating for the recipient.

Another important factor to note is that unlike traditional bullying it can happen at any time of the day or night and it can reach a huge audience very quickly.

"One of the most insidious aspects of it is the permanence of the expression. It also acts as a constant reminder for the victim as every time they log onto a particular website the phrase or remark is there in black and white."
Dr Shane Gallagher, educational and child psychologist

One difference between traditional bullying and cyber-bullying is that bystanders, who would not ordinarily have been involved, are often drawn in. For example, somebody might inadvertently click on to a new Facebook group which has been set up for the specific purposes of bullying somebody and comment without thinking.

Cool or cruel – who decides?

Jonathan is a 15-year-old boy from a close-knit, caring and IT-literate family. Their computer is in the family room, they have set up parental controls with time and content restrictions and he has freedom to use the internet within agreed boundaries. By all accounts they are doing everything right.

Like many teenagers Jonathan has a Facebook profile and he has managed to accumulate 500 friends. One evening a new group appeared titled 'randomer' (youth speak for 'outsider'). He innocently clicked on the group to see what it was about and was shocked to find a manipulated image portraying a boy at his school in a really horrible way.

"Niall had a reputation for always wanting to be part of the cool crowd but everybody thought he was trying too hard. He was always trying to butt into conversations or doing silly things in class," Jonathan explains. "He wasn't very popular."

But did he deserve this? "People started commenting on the page. Some people thought it was really funny and wanted to keep the group going but others said it was really harsh."

What nobody who logged on to the page bargained for was the police turning up at school. Everybody who had signed into the group was called in and questioned about their involvement and had to make a police statement.

How common is cyber-bullying?

The UK charity Beatbullying asked almost 2,500 young people about cyber-bullying. It found that:

- 50% said they had been cyber-bullied
- 29% told no-one about being cyber-bullied
- 73% said they knew who was sending them bullying messages
- 11% admitted to being a cyber-bully.

At the moment cyber-bullying is more common among teenagers, but with ever younger children accessing the internet, even primary school head teachers are seeing incidents of aggression using internet technologies.

> *"Children feel they can be bolder on the internet and find themselves saying things they would never say face to face as they cannot see the reaction of the person [the disinhibition factor]. We have seen a rise of this sort of behaviour at our school."*
> *Jacqui, a primary school head teacher*

The disinhibition factor

This describes the ability to show less concern for somebody than would normally be expected in real life. When a child is sitting at a screen, for example, and cannot see the impact of their behaviour on another, they may have more courage to make hurtful comments. This is made worse because chat rooms encourage pseudonyms and it is possible to create false email addresses.

But so-called 'disinhibition' can also be positive, allowing people with no voice in the real world to express themselves. For example, often children who come from very oppressive families or even very shy children will find an outlet online.

The legal position

Some US states have introduced legislation aimed at penalising cyber-bullying. But in the UK cyber-bullying is not a specific criminal offence. However, there are some laws that could apply to cyber-bullying. Here is a list of what is available.

- All UK state schools are required to have anti-bullying policies under the School Standards and Framework Act 1998 and independent schools have similar obligations under the Education (Independent Schools Standards) Regulations 2003. These should include policies and processes for dealing with cyber-bullying against teachers, as well as pupils.
- Although cyber-bullying is not a specific criminal offence in UK law, criminal laws such as the Protection from Harassment Act 1997 and the Crime and Disorder Act 1998 may apply in terms of harassment or threatening behaviour.
- Where mobile bullying is concerned, the Telecommunications Act 1984 makes it a criminal offence to make anonymous or abusive calls and, if you are harassed persistently on your mobile, it may be an offence under the 1997 Protection from Harassment Act.
- The Communications Act 2003 makes it a criminal offence to send "by means of a public electronic communications network, a message or other matter that is grossly offensive or of an indecent, obscene or menacing character".[36]

Preventing cyber-bullying

As with normal bullying, you can have an impact on how your child acts, and deals with situations. Once again, it's all to do with communication.

- Talk to your children about cyber-bullying and the importance of being kind online.

- Discourage them from posting information about friends which may be construed as negative or commenting on negative remarks by other people.
- Encourage your child to use online groups that are moderated.

A little gossip goes a long way

One of the most shocking instances of mass cyber-bullying erupted in late 2010 when LittleGossip.com was launched. The website encouraged anonymous postings of gossip – but using the real names of the people who were talked about – and people were asked to rank this as true or false.

The majority of postings were extremely cruel and many were openly racist or homophobic. Its popularity grew rapidly with students throughout the UK, and many schools were faced with another sort of bullying to contend with – where they didn't know who the perpetrators were.

The National Union of Teachers accused the site's creators of creating a "vehicle for cyber-bullying", and schools banned the website and sent letters home to warn parents.

The site attracted such an outcry in the media and from schools, parents and anti-bullying charities that it was forced to close in February 2011. However, in June 2011 it relaunched and was very much alive and well. Other incarnations have been created, including plentyofgossip.com.

Surely this is cyber-bullying at its worst.

Recognising the signs of cyber-bullying

- Your child may become withdrawn or appear isolated.
- Their schoolwork may have started to suffer.
- They may appear anxious or distressed after receiving a text message or going online. Some children may be embarrassed

that they are being bullied and take measures to hide their online activity.

- They may abruptly stop using a device or change their pattern of computer usage.
- In a worst case scenario this can lead to depression and even suicide.

What can you do if your child is being cyber-bullied?

As always, communication is important – and given that cyber-bullying is on the rise, equipping your child with the tools to deal with it is essential.

- Learn how to block cyber-bullying messages – this is considered the most effective approach.
- Never respond to abusive messages that are sent by text, instant message, email or in chat rooms. That is what the bully wants and in the heat of the moment your child might say something that could later be used against them.
- Keep a record of all messages – in other words learn how to save text messages and correspondence in chat rooms.
- Learn how to print or save the screen the offending message has appeared on.
- Do not forward offensive messages.

Children mentoring children

One innovative approach to cyber-bullying has been established by the charity Beatbullying. The key to the success of the CyberMentors programme (www.cybermentors.org.uk) is that young people help other young people.

It provides a social network where 17 moderators are online from 8am to 2am, seven days a week for people to talk through their experiences. The website has had over a million unique users since its launch in 2009. Around 3,600 CyberMentors and over a thousand senior mentors have been trained.

Mentoring can be done in a range of different ways – it can be face to face in one of the 250+ schools that have signed up to it, but it can also be online in a safe virtual environment.

Why do children cyber-bully?

Before you can start having any conversation with your child about this new-age menace it is worth trying to understand why children might become cyber-bullies. According to some recent research:

- 81% think it is funny
- 64% do not like the person
- 45% view the victim as a loser
- 59% think cyber-bullying is no big deal
- 47% think there will be no tangible consequences
- 45% think they won't get caught.[37]

Many of us are quick to blame the technology, but this is a social problem and is much better addressed with social solutions. Such solutions need to involve policymakers, e-safety bodies, schools and most importantly parents and their children.

What if your child is the cyber-bully?

It will come as a blow to all parents if you discover your child has been involved in cyber-bullying. As mentioned, cyber-bullying makes it is increasingly easy for children to be involved as they easily become bystanders. So while your child may not ever bully someone in a playground, they may find themselves inadvertently bullying someone online. As parents, we have a duty to educate our children about behaving appropriately – bullying another person is not acceptable.

Among the prevention strategies suggested for cyber-bullying are:

- no access to social networking sites
- confiscation of computers and mobile phones
- setting clear rules and enforcing penalties
- a written school policy on zero tolerance – enforced by exclusion if appropriate
- in severe cases, 20 hours of community service imposed by a relevant authority.

Teacher abuse

It is not always the child who is being bullied and there have been rising numbers of cases where teachers have been at the sharp end of cyber-abuse. This may also have unwanted consequences for your child.

Educational psychologist Teresa Bliss describes one case where a very bright GCSE student had created a website specifically for the purposes of bullying a teacher through the site and her art work. "She was on track to getting an A in the subject but she made the mistake of adding tag lines to her art work which enabled the authorities to establish that she was the bully. The result was that she was not allowed to use the offending art work in her GCSE."

As with all bullying, it is important to remember that cyber-bullies can be victims too. They may be having problems at home – perhaps if their parents' relationship is in difficulty, or perhaps they are having their own personal crisis.

This is where restorative justice could be particularly effective. This is a process which allows all the parties involved to talk about why something happened and how the other person might feel. It gives the people involved the opportunity to explore the reasons why something has happened and can also bring home to the cyber-bully that there is a real person with feelings on the receiving end of nasty messages.

Part 3

What our children really do online

Whether our children are social networking, gaming, instant messaging or creating their own content, one thing is certain: the speed at which the internet is changing and new services are being launched means that what they are doing online will be constantly changing.

On Facebook alone you can play games, chat, upload content and send messages – and no doubt more services will be added soon. A game is no longer just a game your son plays against himself; many games now have a social networking element. One of the most significant developments for parents is the arrival of the mobile internet and the smartphones and tablet devices it can be accessed from. This has a huge impact on how our children use technology and how they are using it at an ever younger age.

Many of us may have embraced new technologies and understood the importance of internet safety, but are still perplexed by how our children are using some services. For example, while most parents will use Facebook to connect or network with people we already know or have lost touch with, many children see it as a way to meet new 'friends' and expand their social circle.

> *"I use Facebook and Twitter but when it comes to my son,*
> *I still feel this is unchartered territory. I can't turn to my own*
> *parents to ask what they would have done in their day. And*
> *the world of my childhood was certainly a very different*
> *place to the one my son is growing up in."*
> **Anne, mum to James (9)**

One thing is certain: social networking has now reached a mass audience and our children are part of that too. So whether they are adding friends on Facebook, sliding down the snow-covered slopes of Club Penguin or battling it out on the football fields of Fifa 11, our children are increasingly connecting with other people.

In Part 2 we considered some general rules. Now let us get into detail and look at what exactly our children are doing online.

11

The Facebook phenomenon

It's nigh on impossible not to have heard of Facebook, MySpace or YouTube. We simply cannot escape news about how social networking is changing the world we live in as the Arab spring and looting across UK cities this year has shown. However, while Bebo and MySpace may have paved the way for social networking, Facebook is now the undisputed leader.

Since its launch in 2004, 750 million people around the world have signed up to use Facebook, outstripping the early popularity of Bebo and MySpace which have closer to 100 million users. It seems to be the social networking site of choice for our children too. Like MySpace and Bebo, there is a theoretical age limit of 13 but children – often with their parents' consent – do not think twice about flouting this rule.

FACT   A 2011 CHILDWISE report found that:

- 2 million children under the age of 13 have a Facebook page

- 81% of nine- to 16-year-olds use social networking sites
- 34% of five- to 16-year-olds say Facebook is their favourite website
- two-thirds of all seven- to 16-year-olds have visited a social networking site; three in five have a profile.[38]

How our children use Facebook

How children use Facebook very much depends on the age group. While this social networking site tends to become more popular as children reach the age of ten, research shows that children as young as five have come into contact with some form of social networking. Interestingly, in most cases this is now Facebook, which may be down to the popularity of the site with their parents.

In a survey of 180 nine- to 11-year-olds in London, over a third said Facebook was a useful site to chat with friends, make new friends and talk to family members who live on the other side of the world. Many younger children enjoy Facebook games like Farmville, which allows members to manage a virtual farm.

As children reach 13 they begin to use Facebook to organise their social life and share personal interests with friends. They post information about their own lives, comment on their friends' lives, upload photographs and videos, share their thoughts on new music or films, join groups or networks that interest them and sometimes even set up their own groups. If they are blogging on a site like Tumblr or are active on Formspring (see p134), they may link these to their Facebook page, allowing their 'friends' to closely follow all aspects of their online and offline life.

The basics of Facebook

There are many different ways to communicate on Facebook. Below is a flavour of what you may already be familiar with if you have your own profile.

- 'Inline' privacy controls have been introduced (see section on privacy) which now make it possible to edit a profile page more easily. However, they are not perfect.
- A 'status update' is usually a one- or two-liner which will appear on the child's profile page and in their friends' newsfeed (see below for info on feeds).
- 'Commenting' on other people's status updates is a popular pastime.
- You can 'tag' friends in photos or videos but now you must ask them first (see below for the truth about tagging).
- Users can 'like' a video, photograph or statement posted by somebody else – a tool which marketers make the most of!
- Everybody has a 'wall' which friends often write, or post photographs on and a 'poke' is an online version of a nudge.
- There is Facebook chat, or instant messaging (see p118), a real-time messaging service.
- You can apply for your own Facebook email address.
- Facebook Places allows you to share your exact location with a friend.

Feeds

A mini-feed appears on your child's profile page and will appear to everyone they have authorised to see it. This will include posts on their 'wall' made by others, your child's responses to these and where your child has been tagged in photographs. It is possible to manually delete items from the mini-feeds. Through new privacy settings you can control what is actually published here and who sees it.

Newsfeeds, on the other hand, are from networks or groups that your child has joined, and include the activity of their friends. Sometimes activity even of people they are not friends with will appear on your child's home page. By the same token your child's activity may appear on their friends' – and sometimes friends of friends' – newsfeeds. This may expose your child to inappropriate comments from others in that authorised network, especially if these are older people. This may be of concern if they have older friends who are regularly posting without thinking.

Tagging

Tagging photographs and videos is an increasingly popular way to identify or reference others. Previously it was up to your child to stay on top of if they had been tagged in a photograph doing something silly. Now Facebook has given users more 'inline' control and it may not all be positive. In short the good news is: when a 'friend' tags you in a photograph you are now sent a message saying: 'Sally added a photo of you. To approve this for your profile, review your pending posts.' If your child rejects it, the photograph won't appear on his profile and his name won't be 'tagged' to it. The bad news: the untagged photograph will still appear on his friend's profile who is under no obligation to remove it – although you can now send a message asking them to. Worse still is that new privacy settings make it possible – and easier – for a friend to block your child from seeing the offending photo on their own profile and can tag it with any malicious name they see fit without your child being any the wiser. Geotechnology is now embedded in most smartphones, adding a further dimension to this as photos tagged on the move can reveal the exact location of a user (page 145).

Facebook apps

Applications or 'apps' on Facebook are software programmes from third-party websites and have caused a great deal of controversy around privacy and information sharing. At the time of going to press there were over 550,000 Facebook apps.

- Apps allow Facebook users to share bits of information about each other. Many of these access basic information and friends' lists, and then share this with outside companies. Some even collect personal information about users' friends.
- Most users are oblivious to the fact that they have downloaded an app.
- A list of apps that have been downloaded can be found in the privacy section of your account. These will explain just how much your child might be sharing with marketers.
- Apps can also be spam. The 'stalk your ex' or 'who is viewing my profile' variety are examples.
- It is possible to delete apps and switch them off altogether.

Deleting your account

Deleting a Facebook account permanently is now possible but the company holds on to all your details just in case you wish to return, unless you specifically request that these are deleted. Remember, too, that your child's digital footprint (see p45) will be left on other friends' pages. Deleting wall posts or comments is possible but only from your own page.

Security settings

To stop your child's profile being hacked into, or 'fraped' (see p96), Facebook has a number of security settings in place which you have to opt into. As well as the usual security questions and answers, there are a number of different methods, which you can view if you search for 'security features'. To make some of these security measures possible, Facebook requires your mobile phone number (which you have to opt *out* of displaying on your profile).

- **Login notifications and approval** – if you are logging in using a different computer than usual, Facebook will send you a text message with a security code in it, so that you can verify your identity.
- **One-time passwords** – Facebook will send you a different password to your mobile every time you want to log in, meaning

it's impossible to steal someone's password (unless you also steal their mobile).
- **Secure browsing** – this opt-in security feature makes all your activity encrypted, making it harder for anyone else to access your Facebook information without your permission.

Privacy

If any website has come under the media spotlight for its privacy policies, it's Facebook. Given its huge and growing popularity this is unsurprising, and positive, but many would argue with such a huge following it is still not going far enough – especially when it comes to minors. Its latest move to 'inline' controls to the profile page supposedly makes it easier to decide who sees what you post and to remove posts and photographs more easily. Previously this had to be done through a series of settings pages.

These new controls are not perfect and some argue that they may in fact make it easier to cyber-bully somebody and then 'hide' what is being said from them. One of the biggest criticisms is that 'tagging' and 'Facebook places' is now embedded in the control panel of 'status updates'. And this makes it easier to tell people where you, what you are doing and with whom.

One thing is certain, there is no room for complacency and Facebook will no doubt continue to revise its policies but parents should remain involved (see www.facebook.com/safety).

Privacy settings for under-18s

Facebook is clear that the site is not for under-13s but that age verification (see p156) should be the joint responsibility of parents, schools and the industry itself. So in fact it does little to actively enforce this rule.

However, the settings for under-18s are slightly more restrictive than those for adults. This came about because of EU child protection measures and happens automatically. The current situation is that if a minor chooses to share information with the 'public', at most they will be sharing it with 'friends', 'friends of friends' and members of a verified school or work network or group they have joined. Remember that this may run into hundreds of people, some of whom they may not know at all. The use of applications and games on Facebook can be viewed too. However, minors are also opted out of sharing information with public search engines, but that could change.

The real problems arise when under-13s are lying about their age to the extent that they say they are over 18.

> *"Julia, 9, nagged for so long that I eventually let her open a Facebook account. What I didn't know was that she has entered her age as 23. A few weeks later, when I went in to check her profile page, I realised she was being subjected to a whole lot of inappropriate advertising, not to mention friend requests."*
> **Christina, mum to Julia (9)**

When children present themselves as over 18, then EU child protection safety measures become meaningless. These include protecting minors from inappropriate advertising and limiting their ability to be found in public search engines.

A profile page is only as private as your child makes it – in other words it is the user's responsibility to change the settings. Posting their address, email address or date of birth is never a good idea.

Facebook's default setting is that status, photos and posts, biography, favourite quotations and the information you have entered on family and relationships are made public so it is up to the user to change those settings to be made visible to friends, or friends or friends. It is possible to customise this further to make it available to even smaller, select groups.

> TIP When sharing a post, video or photograph, think about who might view it. Always respect another person's request to remove their photograph. Check out www.facebook.com/safety for more information on the company's policy.

The age limit issue

The minimum age for Facebook is 13. Facebook does not actively enforce this rule. Facebook strongly advises minors of 13 years or older to ask their parents for permission before sending any information about themselves to anyone over the internet.

How easy is it for a child under 13 to be on Facebook?

It is very easy for a child under 13 to set up a Facebook profile. All they have to do is fill out their name and email address and give a false date of birth – it is as simple as that. If they give their real date of birth a message comes up stating that they are not eligible to use this service, but then they can just alter the date.

If Facebook learns that information has been collected from children under 13 its stated policy is to 'delete that information as quickly as possible'. The powers that be also invite anybody to contact them if they are aware of an under-age child posting information. However, with 2 million under-13s now on Facebook in the UK it is clear that they are not monitoring under-age use. Facebook simply does not have the staff to do so and if any under-age child was compromised they would probably use the defence that 'ultimate responsibility rests with the parents'.

Despite the age restrictions there are still parents – and responsible parents at that – who will allow their under-13s to use the site.

Should children under 13 be on Facebook?

While many parents have no problem with it, the experts agree that it is a bad idea.

"Facebook states clearly that it is not suitable for children under 13. Many parents are colluding with their children to lie about their age and this is a real problem."
John Carr, adviser to the UK Government and United Nations on child online safety

"No. Social networks were not created for young children. And Facebook, in particular, has not been designed with young children in mind."
Dr Elena Martellozzo, criminologist

"No. It is not sensible to be using an online service in breach of its stated rules. They are commencing their use of social networking with a lie and that is never a good idea."
Rik Ferguson, director of security, research and communication, EMEA Trend Micro

"No. There is a reason the age limit is set at 13 and this is because Facebook can't control the conversations or content that appears which may be difficult for somebody under the age of 13 to cope with. A problem may also arise when children later try to change their date of birth on Facebook. Future employers may question what else they have lied about."
Graham Jones, internet psychologist

"No. There is absolutely no way I would let my son on Facebook without making sure his privacy settings were set to the highest levels. It wasn't stated HR policy but my last employer vetted a potential employee's Facebook activity before even granting a job interview."
Cathy, HR manager and mum to James (9)

By the time they are 13, if not before, the reality is that most children will probably want to try Facebook even if their parents think otherwise.

Ultimately it comes down to parental choice and responsibility and the numbers of under-13s online suggest that many parents are okay with it. We are not endorsing it but if your under-13 is on Facebook then at the very least you should:

1. open your own Facebook account so you can be their friend
2. know their password
3. regularly check activity on the account
4. ensure privacy settings are at the highest levels (see p90)
5. ensure they display no personal information or photographs unless you are okay with it
6. vet any new friends before they are accepted
7. and the same goes for applications and games
8. have a discussion about any posts made on the wall or any comments they have 'liked'
9. remind them of the importance of being kind online.

Even after doing all of the above, your child will be vulnerable to commercial messages targeted at under-18s.

Parents should also be aware that if we deny our children access once they *have* reached 13, they will find a way to set up an account, or their friends will do it for them.

> "My mum didn't want me to have a Facebook account so I just set one up using a false name. My friends all know my false name and I delete my history whenever I use Facebook at home and I've met up with a few people that I met on Facebook."
> **Min Lee, 15**

It seems that draconian measures do not work and by not being aware of your child's account and not understanding what they are doing on Facebook you could be putting them at even greater risk.

This is especially true when they start adding 'friends' they barely know, if at all.

The pitfalls of Facebook

Facebook can be great fun. In the majority of cases it is not 'dangerous' for a child to be on Facebook, but there are some risks you should be aware of, and unwanted consequences of this social network.

New friends online

We are said to be lucky if we can count our true friends on one hand. With the hindsight of experience, most parents will know that real friendship takes time and effort and is based on trust.

Facebook has certainly helped to redefine the word 'friend'. Indeed, there is a strong desire for children to rack up the numbers of friends they have and quite often that number is seen as the measure of popularity in a school group.

> "Having loads of friends is really important, especially for popular girls – it is a kind of status symbol. Some really want to have over a thousand friends. You definitely get more friends by putting up images or videos of yourself showing a bit too much flesh. But you can also get a bad reputation for this."
> **Alika, 16**

For our children, Facebook is a place to 'meet' new friends. A European survey found that:

- four in ten of UK nine- to 16-year-olds have looked for new friends on the internet
- 32% have added contacts they have not met face to face
- 11% have sent an image of themselves to someone they have not met before.[39]

It is really important that your child understands that adding people you do not know can have unwanted consequences. CEOP states clearly that most predatory activity starts in social networking sites like Facebook and Windows Live Messenger. (See p13 on the rise of high-risk behaviour.)

Accepting 'friends' you do not really know can be particularly troublesome if a child's privacy settings are too open and their new 'friend' starts posting inappropriate images or content.

> *"Some guy sent me a friend request. I didn't recognise him but guessed I had met him at a party the previous weekend so I added him without thinking. A few days later he started posting obscene messages about me on my wall. I'd never even met him. It was really annoying so I blocked him."*
> **Kiera, 15**

Blocking someone

Blocking or 'unfriending' certain people is possible. But this also means that if a child is savvy enough they can block you – yes, you the parent – from seeing some of what they are posting. If you block somebody or 'unfriend' them, they will not be notified.

'Fraping', or Facebook raping

People your child actually does know can be a problem too. 'Fraping' is when somebody either has intentionally hacked into your page or has got hold of your password. This happens because friends will use each other's mobile phones to access the social network. If they then forget to sign out this leaves them vulnerable. Sometimes this is done as a joke by people you know but increasingly so-called 'friends' will hack into Facebook and post unpleasant things on each other's sites. Depending on the nature of the incident – and the child – this can be very distressing, not to mention embarrassing.

Nowhere to hide

Lily, 15, was a successful grammar school student. She was gifted both academically and on the sports field and had a boyfriend.

One day she shared on Facebook that she was pregnant. As it turns out, somebody had hacked into her account and had put this message up. Lily did not return to school the following term. Her parents said she had been too distressed by the rumour-mongering that followed the so-called 'frape'.

What was disturbing, says Christine, a teacher at the school, is that many of the younger members of staff seemed to find the incident amusing. And worse still, her classmates admitted that Facebook would be used to let people at Lily's new school know that she was not liked.

Party disasters

A common Facebook horror story for parents is when a child posts that they are throwing a party and includes details like the date, time and address.

"My friend Tania had over 200 'friends'. She was having a party to celebrate her 15th birthday and put the date and address on Facebook. She did not expect all her friends to forward the invite to others. Hundreds of people turned up at her house. Her parents nearly killed her."
Jo, 15

On a more insidious level, your child could receive an invitation and decide to attend, for example, a party where drugs will be readily available. Caitlin was sent several invitations to methadone parties.

Facebook 'addiction'

Perhaps less worrying – but not to be ignored – is that this can also be incredibly time-consuming. Anybody who has spent any time on Facebook will see how easy it is to get lost wandering aimlessly through endless posts, photographs and videos with no particular objective in mind. This could have an impact on whether your child is giving their homework their full attention (see p50 for ways of establishing rules).

> *"Most people have Facebook open in the background when they are doing their homework and flip back and forth to see if there are any new notifications."*
> *Jim, 15*

Where risk-taking manifests itself

In Chapter 2 we discussed how many of the problems our children face online are generated by children themselves. Facebook is a place where this is happening more than ever.

Self-taken, overtly sexual images of under-age children on Facebook are a growing concern for CEOP, which says teenagers – especially girls – do not understand the risks posed to them online by sexual predators.

Should you open an account to keep an eye on your child?

Over 40% of the UK population is now on Facebook so many of you will already have an account. But if you haven't, should you open one? The short answer, if your child has or wants one, is yes.

By opening your own account you can go through the motions of understanding how to make your settings as private as possible.

This will help you understand exactly what your child encounters, and just how public or private information can be. Going through the site's privacy policy and working out how to alter your account settings is a very useful exercise too. Even if you already have an account, reviewing your own privacy settings is worth doing. Many people are unaware of how much information they are displaying and who can view it.

Frankly speaking, the only way you can fully understand how Facebook works, its positives and its negatives, is to use it yourself.

Should you be your child's friend on Facebook?

This is a tricky one. Some parents rightly believe that teenagers need their privacy. Their argument is that they would not expect to listen in to their telephone conversations, read their child's diary or be with them in the playground at all times.

> "No way. I absolutely do not want to be my 16-year-old's friend on Facebook. There are some things that parents should not know. In fact when his nan wanted to add him recently I told him to just ignore the request."
> **Clive, dad to Judith (18), Lyle (16) and Anna (10)**

Others argue that this is not comparing like with like. The argument is that it is not necessary for a parent to monitor a child in the playground because this is a controlled environment. After all, anybody let into the school to work closely with schoolchildren must be police-checked – even parents of children at the school. But on Facebook children can add 'friends' and begin interacting with strangers who are not scrutinised in the same way. Other examples are that a diary cannot be viewed by hundreds of people and a telephone call tends to disappear into the ether, unlike words posted online which are potentially immortalised.

> *"You absolutely should be your child's friend on Facebook.*
> *You should be able to view their online space just like you*
> *can see the mess in their rooms. Our job as parents is to*
> *help them to act appropriately in these public spaces."*
> **Marian Merritt, internet security advocate at Norton**

Ask your child if they would mind being friends with you. In a worst-case scenario they may refuse.

Alternatives to Facebook

For under-13s, **Togetherville** is probably the closest thing young children are going to get to a Facebook-type experience. US-based and now owned by Disney, the site touts itself as a safer social networking experience for under-tens with hopes to extend this to under-13s. **Familyclick** is aimed at pre-school children and specifically at families separated by distance.

For older children (tweens and teens), websites like **Imbee**, **Yoursphere** and **Everloop** are being sold as safer 'trendy' social networking sites where teens and tweens can meet, chat, share videos and so on.

Will any of these be the answer to Facebook? The jury is out. Many argue that websites that require your mother to be looking over your shoulder will surely fail.

Six useful parenting tips for Facebook

1. Set up your own Facebook account to see what it is about and learn how the settings work. You might want to ask your teen to help you do this. This will give you a clear idea of how to start a discussion, and you can raise questions about the privacy of your account that they may not have thought of for theirs.

2. If you insist on being your teenager's friend on Facebook and if you have a problem with their Facebook activity, speak to them about it in the real world.
3. Make sure your child is aware of what the privacy settings mean, and if age-appropriate (and not condescending), ask if you can go on their profile together and choose their settings.
4. Talk to your child about what is appropriate to put on Facebook and what is not.
5. Pick your battles. If a tricky teen is refusing to moderate comments on Facebook, try at least to agree that they alter privacy settings to limit the damage.
6. Keep delivering the message. It is really important for parents to keep talking to their children about what they are doing online and especially on a site that is so popular and changing as rapidly as Facebook.

"Even when teenagers have got to the eye-rolling stage you should keep delivering the messages. Some of it will continue to sink in even if it doesn't feel like it."
Marian Merritt, internet security advocate at Norton

TIP The much-anticipated Google+ – Google's answer to social networking – may put a dent in Facebook's global domination, but only time will tell.

12

Virtual reality and online gaming

Not so long ago, knowing what game your child was playing was pretty straightforward. They may have been in the back of a car with a hand-held device like a Gameboy or in the family room using a games console like the Xbox 360.

But the gaming market, worth over $60 billion, continues to change rapidly. With affordable broadband, games previously only played on a console can be played using a web browser so children can go online on the Xbox, for example, to live 'chat' with other gamers anywhere in the world. At the same time there are many new virtual worlds aimed at children which do not require parents to buy a games console. In addition, the rapid growth of web-enabled mobile gaming means that children can now play anywhere on any device providing there is an internet connection. All this has helped make gaming far more accessible and much harder to walk away from.

What does this mean for our children? Undoubtedly gaming, in whatever form, is one of the most popular activities for children, with 83% of UK nine- to 16-year-olds playing games in some form or other.[40] Just consider the user numbers on some of the most popular online virtual worlds for children, or check out the best-selling console games, for proof. Most of these online games offer some level of free play but there are usually premium memberships to access more exclusive benefits – for these, parents will have to get out the credit card.

Chances are that if you have a younger child hooked in the online world, there will be gimmicks available for purchase in the real world too. Many toys for children now have online worlds – Build A Bear, Barbi, Lego and Bratz, to name but a few. For those games that started life in cyberspace, having real-world products seems to be a sign of arrival (see p19).

> *"Moshi is starting to become really cool now. You can buy Moshi stuff from the shops."*
> **Niamh, 10**

Our worries about gaming are compounded by endless negative stories in the media about how computer games are addictive and can encourage violent, racist or other antisocial behaviour.

> *"I connect with loads of people around the world when I am playing Call of Duty. Sometimes people say racist things and sometimes I get these weird blogs and links to websites. I showed my sister some of the weird ones and she told me to shut them down."*
> **Peter, 13**

But can games actually be good for our children? We take a look at how to help your child actually benefit from game time on p115. First, let's look at how to ensure the games your child is playing are as safe as possible.

Game boys

It would appear that more boys play console games than girls.

- 92% of all children live in a household with a games console.

- Boys aged five to 15 are more likely than girls to live in households with a games console, and this applies across all age groups. This consistent divide between boys and girls across each age group is not evident for any other type of media in the home.

- Boys show a much higher daily use of games consoles, spending around 147 minutes a day playing, in contrast to the 50 minutes a day spent by the girls.[41]

Choosing a virtual world

There are thousands of games for your child to choose from, whatever their interest. If you google the phrase 'online games for children', expect close to 200 million responses. Among the most popular of these are virtual worlds where children create an avatar, earn currency and complete a puzzle or quest. These usually involve some degree of social networking.

Some gaming terminology

An **avatar** is your child's online representation of himself. In most online games, they choose a character and then adapt it according to how they wish to look – this can range from a bloodied soldier to a cute boy or girl wearing, well, very little, or something as benign as a chubby penguin.

Virtual worlds is a term which can be applied across a range of services, from specific gaming worlds like World of Warcraft or communities using console gaming platforms (Xbox Live, PlayStation Network and so on) to simulated real-world environments. Essentially they are an online playground where children can create an avatar and complete various quests while chatting to old and new friends in real time.

Role-playing games (RPGs) are where the player controls one party or several in a group to complete a quest. **MMORGs** are massive multiplayer online role-playing games.

Questions to ask about online games

Over the years, because of increased pressure by the media, the gaming industry, parents and governments, online gaming sites have had to take safety and privacy seriously.

Some are certainly doing a better job than others, but there is still work to be done and we as parents can play a crucial role in upping the bar by actively engaging in the worlds our children enter and getting involved in what they are doing.

Many websites for children – especially younger ones – now require a parental email address to open an account. Here are some of the things you should consider before letting your child loose in a virtual world.

Is it COPPA-compliant?

Many websites originate in the US where its laws apply. As such they should comply with the US Children's Online Privacy Protection Act (COPPA) of 2000. This says that if you operate a commercial website or online service directed to children under the age of 13 which collects personal information from them, or if you operate a general audience website and have actual knowledge that you are collecting personal information from children, you must comply with this Act.

Does the website display any recognised privacy seal such as Safe Harbor, Privo or TRUSTe?

These are a sign that websites are adhering to appropriate marketing regulations, which are stringent for children's websites. They are also a signal that privacy controls are appropriate for children and the site is deemed a 'healthy' place to be. These seals should be prominently displayed, preferably on the home page.

How is chat regulated?

Websites should use a technology solution which automatically flags up inappropriate language or exchanges but there should be human moderation too for context. With many user lists running into millions, human moderation alone is simply not enough. Be wary of 'community-moderated chat'. This is where the site relies only on users to report inappropriate behaviour – it is increasingly accepted that many users simply do not report.

Is the chat free or pre-scripted?

Free chat means the child can use his own words; pre-scripted chat is where the child has a set of questions and responses to choose from. For younger users pre-scripted chat is recommended.

Has the website created its own whitelists or blacklists?

When it comes to online chat, a site with a blacklist will filter certain negative, unacceptable words that have been defined by the website's owner. For example, if a user types 'screw you', this would appear as '***** you'.

A whitelist site has created its own limited dictionary, so *all* words *not* in the dictionary will be blocked. So if you typed 'screw you' it would not be allowed through. A user can post only what is in the whitelist's dictionary, thus limiting the content, and excluding any inappropriate content.

No technical solution can ever be perfect, but a site using a blacklist would never block 'sssssssccccc-rrrreeewwwww yyyyoooooouuuu', whereas a whitelisted site would. See p59 about using black- and whitelists in your computer software.

Does the site allow third-party advertising?

Even though advertising might be strictly regulated for children, ask yourself whether you want your child exposed to marketing messages.

Does the website's payment system have checks and balances in place to limit overspending?

Do they keep your credit card details when you purchase a membership and how easy is it to overspend?

What filtering and monitoring solutions does the site have?

Many websites are signing up to use what is called a 'community management platform' by Crispthinking.com. It is the system used by the biggest names in the online world, including Lego, Sony Online Entertainment and Cartoon Network. Moshi Monsters and Pora Ora have recently invested in it.

> *"We have recently invested in Crisp software which is the holy grail in online safety. In nanoseconds it can go through gazillions of lines of chat and flag things up in prioritised lists for human moderators. It sees what the human eye would never, ever see."*
> **Rebecca Newton, chief community and safety officer, at Mind Candy, the company behind Moshi Monsters**

What is the educational content on the site and what did the game designer have in mind?

What skills is your child developing? For example, is there parental feedback on how well your child is doing with the skills-based puzzles or tasks? In the recently launched Pora Ora, parents can receive feedback on their child's level of performance against national expectations.

How detailed is the safety information on the site?

Look out for active parent communities coupled with good information for parents. Club Penguin does this well and on Moshi Monsters there is a very active parent community. Pora Ora also rates parental involvement highly.

Popular online games

Here are some of the most popular online games for children, and a rundown of what they offer, as well as any potential issues with the games, from the list above.

MoshiMonsters.com (50 million users; ages 5–12)

Adopt a pet monster, name it, choose a cool colour and then develop its personality. Lavish it with attention and gifts and the livelier, friendlier and happier it will become. Complete a daily puzzle, post on the pin board, add friends to a friends' tree and earn Rox, the in-game currency to buy your monster gifts. One in two UK children now has a Moshi account. Owned by Mind Candy.

Pros: No real-time chat. Instead the site uses other social networking features like blogs, pin boards, newsfeeds and buddy lists. There is only one puzzle to complete a day so children don't go into the 'black hole' when they spend too long playing and cannot be dragged away. Uses the latest software and has human moderators for context. No third-party advertising.

Cons: Could be hard on the pocket as there is plenty to buy in the online store. Expect to be harassed by your child for a membership and real-world goods.

ClubPenguin.com (28 million users; ages 6–14)

Users create a penguin avatar and waddle around a snow-filled island inhabited by Puffles, natives to the island (and available for purchase). Acquired by Disney in 2007.

Pros: Chat can be set to pre-scriptive chat. There is a big focus on e-safety and a strong parent community. No adverts of third-party products.

Cons: Free chat is possible. To access exclusive games, parties and events and the ability to buy more than two Puffles you must be a member. Expect to be hassled for a membership as most of the really cool features require one.

Poptropica.com (70 million users; ages 6–15)

Avatars travel from island to island, changing costumes and collecting a special medal after every completed quest. Published by the Family Education Network, a part of Pearson, an education, services and technology company.

Pros: Only pre-scriptive chat available. Prides itself on being educational – children play games and can read books and comics.

Cons: You need a membership to really get the benefits.

Stardoll.com (30 million users; ages 7–17)

A favourite with girls, this Swedish outfit is the internet's answer to paper dolls. Adopt a doll and start to express yourself with a new hairstyle. Change outfits and accessories to perfect a look and even give a favourite celebrity a makeover.

Pros: Girls love to role-play with dolls and can do this here with others who have a similar interest in fashion. Good for those with an interest in design.

Cons: Encourages materialism so you'll need some Stardoll currency. Got into trouble for inappropriate marketing a few years back but has now cleaned up its act. Expect to see adverts from well-known brands.

Habbo.com (203 million users; ages 13–17)

In the world's biggest online hotel, teenagers create an avatar to socialise with their friends and then design their own space to chill out in. There are public and private guest rooms for chatting and players can adopt a pet. Habbo is owned by Finnish-based Sulake Corporation in Helsinki.

Pros: Lots of places to visit and plenty of people to chat to all over the world. Offers some useful safety tips (but users tend to ignore them).

Cons: Possibility for some bizarre conversation. Expect to see comments like 'Inyusha likes buttsecks'. Cybersex in private rooms happens. Third-party advertising is allowed. Furniture and in-site products can be bought with real money. Users are relied on to report bad behaviour but they don't. Notorious for the arrest of a teenager in 2007 who stole nearly £3,000 of virtual furniture bought with real cash.[42]

Neopets.com (50+ million users; any age)

Founded by a Brit back in 1999, Neopets has enabled visitors to Neopia to create their own virtual pets, earn Neopoints by doing well in games or acquiring Neocash with real money. This was one of the first websites to use something called immersive advertising (the integration of advertising into a site's content). Owned by Viacom, the world's fourth biggest media company.

Pros: Plenty to do on the site – play games, care for your pet, solve puzzles, play the stock market.

Cons: No specific age range, so adults and children play together. May encourage gambling. Allows third-party advertising and marketing.

PoraOra.com (aiming for 30 million users; under–14s)

Take your personalised avatar and its Pora Pal, your own virtual pet, on a wild and wonderful adventure in the Starlite world. Based in Ireland, the whole premise of this is learning while having fun. Developed by Caped Koala Studios.

Pros: Parents can receive reports on how well their child is progressing against national curriculum targets. Safety and security are a top priority.

Cons: It is still finding its feet, so has very few users.

RuneScape.com (250+ million users; aged 13+)

A fantasy role-playing game where avatars can be customised, this is a MMORG game (see p105) and a popular place for teenagers, especially boys, to meet. Owned by Jagex Ltd.

Pros: In general there is a supportive community. It is free to play – hence the enormous user base. If you buy a membership there are no adverts. Players are set lots of goals and objectives and there are quests to complete and items to acquire which makes it exciting. It uses filters to prevent swearing. When it comes to collecting personally identifiable information about children, parents are able to view what has been collected.

Cons: Violence could be a problem – cold-blooded murder is possible! More than a third of the players are over 19. You may struggle to drag your child away from it. Developed for over-13s but under-13s can play.

World of Warcraft (12+ million users; aged 13+)

This is a multiplayer online role-playing game where a player controls an avatar which is able to cross landscapes while fending off various monsters, completing quests while interacting with others. Owned by Blizzard Entertainment, an American video game developer.

Pros: Some argue that children can use games like this to acquire important life skills. There is a parental control feature that allows you to set time limits.

Cons: Requires a subscription either through prepaid cards or giving debit or credit card details. Violence could be a problem. It is all-consuming and it can be very hard to stop children playing.

Phishing in virtual worlds

Phishing, the fraudulent use of emails or websites to extract information from somebody, is a common problem on online gaming sites. These attacks begin with a 'phish' to steal login details and end with a virus being sent to your computer which may put banking credentials and other potentially sensitive information at risk. In 2011, a huge phishing attack on Sony hit the media, as 77 million user accounts were compromised – and personal information and credit card details obtained. Neopets has also experienced well-documented cases of phishing attacks.

Hackers target online gaming sites aimed at children, as they are willing to share information more easily.

> "Quite often, the children are used as stepping stones to get to the parents."
> **Christopher Boyd, senior threat researcher, GFI Software**

As well as communicating the risks of sharing too much information online to your child (see p41), here's some specific advice to prevent phishing.

1. There are many forms of malware which specifically look to capture login details used in virtual worlds, especially those where transactions take place. Always ensure that your antivirus software and operating system are up to date.
2. Some virtual worlds allow users to code their own in-world objects, and occasionally this code can perform malicious acts or have strange side effects. Take note of any messages sent by the site's administrator.
3. Many external sites offer to automate and perform menial tasks or services that the account owner doesn't want to do themselves. As these sites require both payment and your login details, there is the risk of both financial and account theft. Treat such services with scepticism.
4. Never download programs that claim to give you free rewards, points or prizes – especially if they ask for login details. These programs are advertised heavily on video-sharing websites.
5. Advise your child never to give login credentials to other gamers in gaming sessions, by either text or voice.

Specific advice for consoles

Quite often parents purchase a games console and then leave the children to it. That is not a good idea. At the very least you should observe the following advice.

1. Familiarise yourself with parental controls specific to your console. Most console manufacturers have dedicated portals on their websites.

2. Consoles often have timers, passwords and privacy options built in – these should be set before allowing the child to go online.

3. If your child wants to make a digital purchase, rather than use and save a parent's credit or debit card details on the console's download service, use either a prepaid funding card specific to your gaming network of choice or a prepaid credit card. These are available from most newsagents, post offices and some banks and allow you to preload a set amount of money, thus capping your child's spending.

"I got my credit card bill to find that several hundred pounds had been spent on Xbox games because I had failed to tick the right box and the website had stored my financial details and I hadn't set a password on the console."
Jack, dad to Connor (14)

Gaming – how much is too much?

If you are worried that your child is spending too much time gaming you are not alone. Our childhoods were so far removed from the experience of our own children that even if we can see and understand the appeal, we cannot help wonder whether all this screen time does them any good.

But it actually may do. Some research[43] – though most of this has admittedly been done on adolescents – shows that if a child plays for two hours a day, chances are they will have a wider circle of friends, be more likely to engage in physical activity and do their homework.

Any more than that and other aspects of a child's life might start to suffer. Children need fresh air, physical activity and the ability to interact in social environments with real people. If they are spending all day playing games, that is not going to happen.

Two hours of screen time a day (and that includes television) is often quoted as an appropriate amount of time. This is, however, increasingly hard to enforce, especially when you consider the range of media available to our children.

Chances are, once you've added in TV time, and checking Facebook, it's more than two hours (remember that statistic that children spend seven hours a day online?).

Gaming addiction

We touched on the risk of addiction on p25 but it is worth restating that only a small minority of children will become truly addicted. Having said this, excessive playing is quite common, and can be problematic. While not technically 'addiction', heavy use could impact on family life and your child's ability to concentrate at school. Try to enforce a 'two hours a day' rule. See p48 for more on setting rules and establishing boundaries.

"Conall and his dad are always on the PlayStation and always 'in the middle of a game'. It is impossible to drag them away from it. The same is not true of Maddie and her DSi – there is never a problem getting her off it."
Shannon, mum to Conall (12) and Madeline (8)

Get the most out of game time

Computer games are here to stay, and children enjoy playing them. So if playing them is inevitable, can your child actually benefit from game time?

Professor Mark Griffiths, of the International Gaming Research Unit at Nottingham Trent University, who has done extensive research into the impact of online gaming on children for over two decades, stresses that appropriate games used in the right context are not inherently bad. They might even be good for our children – the benefits range from social to educational and therapeutic.

Back in 2008, the BBC conducted research[44] into children's experience of virtual worlds and found that these were places where children rehearse what they will do in real life. Unlike television, games involving virtual worlds are not a passive experience and can be very engaging – if used wisely and with appropriate support, they can be a helpful educational tool.

Here are some tips to help your child benefit from game time.

- Get to know – yes, you the parent – what online virtual worlds are out there. If you are not tech-savvy yourself, ask your child to show you how. You may even have fun.
- Content is important – choose educational games over violent games. Like films, games for hand-held devices and consoles come with an age rating on the box. This is not always so clear with online games so it is the parent's responsibility to research this. There are a number of parent-run websites which rank games but ultimately the decision rests with you. Age restrictions are there for a reason so make sure your child is playing age-appropriate games.

  "My five-year-old son was really into playing soldiers in the garden. So I thought for rainy days I'd get him Call of Duty

[certificate 15]. One afternoon he was playing it and I came in to have a look at what he was doing. I didn't realise there were prostitutes in this game."
Erin, mum to Jack (now 6)

- Social is better than solitary – encourage your child to play games that are social and involve interaction with other people. These will help your child to learn to work with other people.
- Manufacturer recommendations are there for a reason – if these say sit two feet from the screen, play in a well-lit room, never have the screen on maximum brightness and never play when tired, then for health reasons alone it is really important that parents ensure this happens.
- Set time limits for playing – see p114.

"David and John [his dad] once played from 10am to 10pm without stopping. I felt there was an issue with behaviour and concentration when they came off it. This resulted in it being confiscated and our family life has improved immeasurably."
Eleanor, mum to David (12) and Erin (8)

> **TIP** US website www.commonsensemedia.org rates and reviews games, films, apps and websites for children. You can search by age range, to find out what is and what isn't suitable for your child, as rated by other parents.

Playing the right games, with the right supervision and restrictions in place, can have some benefits for your child. These include:

- boosting maths skills
- developing literacy if young children are encouraged to read instructions
- sharpening memory and developing critical thinking skills
- encouraging social interaction with other players.

As parents, we've just got to make sure the time our children spend in front of the screen does not get out of hand. Trust your instincts on this one – you'll probably find that attempting this tests your parenting skills to the maximum!

TIP The launch of Pottermore, an online community for fans of the Harry Potter books books, in October 2011 is likely to be the next big thing.

13

IM, email and webcam
The new telephone call?

Instant messaging (IM) services like AIM, Yahoo Messenger, GoogleTalk, Skype, Windows Live Messenger (formerly MSN) or Facebook chat are extremely popular with our children. They love them, and can spend hours talking nonsense to their friends – and strangers. IM poses a much greater risk to our children than gaming – unlike most virtual games, these services have millions of users operating in environments that are completely unmoderated.

The terms of service for all the above mentioned IM services stipulate that the users are over 13. But increasingly, younger and younger children are starting on Facebook and then moving onto Windows Live Messenger, Skype or some other instant messaging service. "These are really not safe for children as they get invites from all sorts of other people," says the ICT co-ordinator of a London primary school.

FACT In the UK, instant messaging (commonly known as IM) and email are still very popular choices for nine- to 16-year-olds, with over 60% using these services to communicate.[45] Interestingly, just a quarter of UK children in this age group use chat rooms but a third use webcams.

IM vs chat – what's the difference?

IM – strictly speaking, this refers to a real-time conversation between two or more people using a text-based service over the internet like Windows Live Messenger. Many of these services now include the ability to talk for free, share files and collaborate using a webcam. Most children will have a so-called **buddy list** which is essentially a list of their contacts. In Facebook, a friends list is used in a similar way.

Chatting – this takes place in groups in a virtual space known as a room and happens between more than two people, quite often strangers. What all chat rooms have in common is that it is possible to exchange messages with countless people at any one time. There are chat rooms that cater for every taste and interest and most chat rooms offer the facility for users to chat privately.

Chat with webcam – these services have exploded as the web has grown and there are now countless websites where you can talk to real people all over the world in real time and see them at the same time. All you need are a webcam and a microphone. Most of these require you to be over 18 but existing age verification processes (see p156) make this meaningless and many children, given the chance, will test them out.

"Certainly no child under the age of 12 has any need to use instant messaging without an adult being there to log them in. And they should certainly not be allowed anywhere near a webcam."
Rebecca Newton, chief community and safety officer at Mind Candy, the company behind Moshi Monsters

By the time most children reach the age of 12, if not before, they will be using an instant messaging service in one form or another. Many of these services now work with webcams and many children are using this technology for collaborative homework.

> *"My friend and I use webcam when we are doing our*
> *homework. It is really cool because it feels a bit like you are*
> *with them."*
> **Louise, 12**

For many children, this is our generation's equivalent of getting home from school and picking up the phone to spend an hour chatting to somebody you just caught the bus home with. If this sounds familiar you can probably also remember your parents asking what on earth you had to talk about.

Some things may not have changed; but IM, of course, is not the same as a telephone call. The downside is that your child can be contacted by strangers at any time or add contacts he may not know. According to CEOP, grooming a child to perform a sexual act and inciting a child to watch a sexual act – both offences – are happening in the main within Windows Live Messenger.

Top tips for parents

To ensure that your child stays safe while using IM, take note of the following advice.

- Be involved. Know what services your child is using. Check these out for content and reputation. If they don't want to tell you, check your browser history but be aware they may have deleted this.
- Get to know their online friends. Parents usually know their children's real-world friends and the same should be true on the internet. Check contact lists regularly to make sure you know everyone they talk to. Unless absolutely necessary, do not do this

behind their back, rather ask them to show you who is in their online crowd.

- Talk to them about being kind online – this cannot be overstated (see Chapter 10 for more on cyber-bullying).
- Encourage your child to tell you if something has made them feel uncomfortable, and if you are not technology-literate learn how to save a conversation or webpage together.
- As they get older, many teenagers will want more freedom. Except in circumstances where there is a clear need, they won't want you hanging over their shoulder reading every message.

TIP Childnet's Chatdanger website (www.chatdanger.com) is aimed at teens and contains real-life stories which may make the dangers of chatting online sink in.

Specific advice for your children using IM or chat rooms

As well as being aware of the risks yourself, help your child understand what they can do to protect themselves while chatting to friends online. Go through the list below with them, and make sure they understand the reasoning behind each point.

- Never complete a personal profile or a member directory profile using your email address or screen name (these profiles are public and can be viewed by anyone using the service). Instead use a nickname and choose this carefully.
- Do not give anybody you meet online – and do not know and trust in the real world – your email address or screen name.
- Carefully review any new buddy list request before allowing somebody to join your circle. Learn how to block an offensive contact.
- Do not use IM to spread rumours or gossip or make rude or cruel remarks in chat rooms.

- Do not use your IM name or email address in any public areas on the internet – this could lead to spam or phishing attacks.
- Never give out personal, sensitive or financial details.
- Never open files or pictures or click on links from people you do not know. In other words treat anything vaguely suspicious, including links from buddies, as spam (see p23).
- Make sure you know how to print a screen to save and keep any offending conversations.

Get to know the lingo

Children have developed their own text-based lingo and it is worth getting to know what some of this means. This will help you decipher conversations if you are worried about your child's online activity.

- A/S/L – age, sex, location
- BF – boyfriend
- DIKU – do I know you?
- F2F – face to face
- GF – girlfriend
- H&K – hug and kiss
- ILU – I love you
- IPN – I'm posting naked
- IWALU – I will always love you
- KOC – kiss on cheek
- KOL – kiss on lips
- LOL – laugh out loud
- LTR – long-term relationship
- NIFOC – naked in front of computer
- NP – nosy parents
- OLL – online love
- P911 – my parents are coming!
- PA – parent alert

- PAL – parents are listening
- PANB – parents are nearby
- PM – private message
- POS – parent over shoulder
- TAW – teachers are watching
- WTGP – want to go private

14

Browsing and downloading
Google, YouTube and iTunes

Googling and browsing

'Google' has become synonymous with searching for information on any imaginable subject. As great as it is, it is also a challenge for parents. Firstly, some of the most innocent phrases can return inappropriate content. But as children get older they start to test boundaries and will enter certain words into search engines out of curiosity. Even young children will google terms they hear in, for example, music videos, which can throw up unwanted content.

> *"I checked my eight-year-old daughter's browsing history and she was googling things like 'hot date' which she heard in the lyrics of some pop song. You don't want to know what she came across!"*
> **Andrea, mum to Lily (8)**

Google is obviously the main search engine but it is not the only one. Yahoo! and Bing (Microsoft's search engine) are the other big names that, like Google, offer email. New ones are springing up all the time.

If your child has an email address with any of the above, they will have an account and in this you can set filters for safe searching. However, these come with no guarantee that inappropriate content will be filtered. After setting the filters try entering a few words with potentially sexual connotations and you will soon get the picture. In spite of this it is strongly recommended that you do set these filters – as they are of some use. These are usually found in account settings or preferences.

> **TIP** Some parents have found that Bing is not suitable for children as the settings are too easy to bypass.

Here are some top tips on browsing safely.

- Help your child set up and then manage all their online accounts.
- Set their search settings. Generally speaking there are three safe search levels. The terms and conditions vary slightly but basically the highest level will filter explicit text, video and images. The next level, moderate, will filter just images and video. Finally there is off – you definitely don't want this one! The default in most searches tends to be moderate.
- Switch off the function that predicts what you are searching for. For example, in Google this is called Google Instant; in Yahoo! it is Search Direct.
- If you sign into a Google account, you can lock the settings to apply Google's strict filtering to all searches from your computer – regardless of whether the person using the computer is signed into this account or not.
- Encourage younger children to use child-friendly search engines such as kids.yahoo.com, www.askkids.com, www.kidzui.com or www.kidsclick.org.

> TIP If you have network-level security (see p66), or
> safety software installed, this will safeguard your
> computer against much inappropriate content, regardless of
> whether your child's account settings are in place – but it's still
> best to do both!

Checking your child's history

All the major web browsers – Firefox, Internet Explorer, Safari (the
default browser for Macs) – allow you to check histories. If they have
a Google or Yahoo! account, histories are also saved here. However, it
is just as easy for your child to delete their history. As they get older,
or if they have something to hide, they will almost certainly know
how to do this – you'll know they've done this if you check and the
history is blank.

All web browsers vary but usually across the top of the page there is
a Tools or History section, where you can check and delete histories
and cookies. It is also possible to manage privacy and security here.
Some browsers, like Internet Explorer, have inbuilt parental controls
(found in Tools>Internet Options) but others, like Firefox, don't.

> TIP In your browser it's possible to turn off predictive
> typing. It's a good idea to do this as it will stop
> innocent searches leading to inappropriate content.

Can you recover a child's history if they have deleted it?

Never say never, but unless you are a real techie or have installed
some kind of key-logging or tracking software this is going to be
difficult. For this reason keeping the lines of communication open
remains our most powerful tool.

Timewasting

If it seems your child is spending too much time online, find out what they are doing. Aimlessly surfing the internet can be a bit of a time waster. Half of our nine- to 16-year-old children are quite happy whiling away time even when they are not particularly interested.

- 42% of children agree that they have caught themselves surfing when they are not really interested.
- 16% say this happens fairly often.[46]

Anybody who is a regular internet user will know how easily one is seduced into wandering aimlessly without any sense of purpose. They will also know just how easy it is to stumble across inappropriate and potentially harmful content.

YouTube

There can be no discussion about our children, teenagers and the internet without mentioning YouTube. Here, children can either watch videos that have been uploaded to the internet or they can post their own.

Given the UK's love of television, it is unsurprising that 75% of children aged nine to 16 watch video clips online and YouTube is an incredibly popular medium.[47] With hundreds of millions of videos uploaded on every subject imaginable, there is plenty of choice – and it is not always suitable for children.

> *"There are a huge number of incredibly entertaining viral shareable videos on YouTube but there is also a lot of content that is not appropriate for children."*
> **Rik Ferguson, director of security, research and communication, EMEA Trend Micro**

Inappropriate images for young eyes

With no safety settings on YouTube, even the most innocent searches throw up content you would rather your young child did not watch.

> "I entered Peppa Pig into the search engine and left my six-year-old to it, only to come back to find she was watching a music video entitled 'WildHearts-Headf**k' [without the censorship]. That came up on the second page."
> **Catherine, mum to Amy (6) and Jack (3)**

YouTube states that the site is for over-13s, despite its popularity with younger children. YouTube's parent resource section states that to create an account, users must confirm that they are at least 13 years old – but of course it's easy to enter a different date of birth.

Videos on YouTube range from the totally innocent to the very disturbing. While YouTube clearly states it is not for pornography and actively removes inappropriate content, there are still clips on there you'd not want your 15-year-old to see, let alone your eight-year-old. Children displaying videos of how to self-harm is just one example, but search on anything potentially controversial or risqué and you will soon get the picture.

Unlike many adults who tend to passively watch videos rather than participate, younger people treat YouTube as just another social network. After watching they may also rate the content, giving it the thumbs up, or down. You'll find the majority of comments left by users on YouTube are very negative, and many contain swear words. This could be seen as cyber-bullying, by people who don't even know you, and is a result of the disinhibition our children experience online (see p75).

The much-loved Justin Bieber, who made his debut on YouTube and is now a global star, gets some pretty cutting comments, despite his popularity. It seems easier for children to give negative rather than positive feedback. Not only is this not nice for your child to read, it may affect them directly should they choose to post videos of their own.

Parent controls on YouTube

Of course, blocking YouTube completely is one way around this issue, but if you apply draconian measures children will only find ways to get around them.

YouTube has an opt-in 'safety mode' which is essentially a content-filtering tool. The safety mode will filter 'potentially objectionable material' and videos with 'mature content' or those that have been age-restricted.

This appears at the bottom of the YouTube page. You can 'lock' this for your browser, meaning that you don't need to be signed into an account for it to work. Anyone using your computer and browser will have these settings applied.

YouTube acknowledges that this filtering tool is not 100% accurate, and relies on users flagging up unsuitable content too. So it's also a good idea to investigate other content filtering software for your PC or network (see Chapter 8).

How to check what your child has been watching

To see your child's viewing history, they must have been signed into an account that you have access to.

- Go to your account page.
- Click the History link in the 'My Videos' section.

Creating video content

It is possible to create video content, also known as 'vlogging', for YouTube or any other network like Facebook or Flickr. However, at the moment research shows our children tend to do this less than watching and commenting.

Someone who experienced the cruelty of the YouTube audience herself was American teenager Rebecca Black, who became a sensation in the USA after recording the song 'It's Friday'. The video went viral and has attracted over 130 million viewers. The negative response was overwhelming: 2.7 million 'dislikes' versus just 376,000 'likes'. Black later admitted on national TV that some of the vitriolic comments had reduced her to tears.

While creating and loading content for the world stage can be problematic, many experts believe that we should be actively encouraging our children to create more and watch less.

If it's good, a video could go viral – as Rebecca Black's did. This is when a video becomes popular very quickly. This could be something funny, political or shocking and usually something that people will react strongly to and want to share with as many people as possible. Quite often the media will pick up on this and it will gather further momentum. If this happens, your child could quickly become the focus of unwanted negative attention.

How to vlog safely

There are some safety measures within YouTube to limit the amount of abuse your child could experience.

- Videos posted can be set to public or private. If a video is public it is open to receiving comments from millions of people, leaving your teenager potentially open to abusive comments. If it is private, only the creator and up to 50 other users who they choose can see the video. The video will also not appear in any search results.
- Make sure the settings are to 'review comments' before they are posted.

Bending the rules – should children under 13 use YouTube?

Charlie, nine, has always loved making videos. He started doing this with the family video camera at about the age of five. For his sixth birthday he was given his own.

At a young age Charlie and his dad made little animations using a website called aniboom.com. By the time he was eight he had decided he wanted to make short films for YouTube. Charlie is under the 13 age limit, but his parents are pretty relaxed about him going online.

"I think everybody worries that their children have too much screen time and I'd like him to read more. But you can't force a child to do anything and I'm happier with him doing something creative than passively watching telly," says his mum, Kim.

However, there are a few rules Charlie must adhere to.

- No laptops in the bedroom.
- Ring dad to ask before downloading anything.
- Promise never to post anything on YouTube before his parents agree.
- Ask his friends and their parents if it is okay before posting anything relating to them online.
- Tell his parents if he stumbles across anything unsuitable – he has once!

"Obviously we facilitate his creativity but he makes the films himself," says Kim. "I was really impressed when he made two separate films and used some sample software to make his own film."

So far he has not had too many comments on his videos but he does tell his friends about his creations. "We should really check if his settings are that we can review comments before they go up. I am not sure how he would feel if people started ridiculing him. And, of course, videos can go viral, which may be a hazard," says his mum. This – and setting and content filtering – is something perhaps they need to think about.

Charlie is fairly unusual. The latest research shows that UK children are much more passive users of technology with most preferring to watch or participate than actually create.

Downloading music

Legally downloading music, as well as film and video, has now become very popular, with the major online outlets being iTunes and Napster. There are other licensed retailers like Amazon, Artist Direct and Bleep and in this fast-changing environment new ones are emerging all the time.

All children love music and if you spend a bit of time listening to lyrics or watching music videos you will quickly understand that their content can be explicit. Now, of course, you can also access the internet via music devices such as the iPod Touch – yet another thing to think about.

So are there any options for parental controls in stores like iTunes or Napster?

Napster's terms of service are that you need to be 18 to enter into an agreement with them, and if you are 13 you must have parental approval. But as this is the internet, there is currently no way of checking this. One limitation is that when parental controls are set this prevents people downloading on Napster – something teenagers love to do.

With an iTunes account where it is possible to buy not only music but film and television programmes too, it is possible to set parental controls in 'preferences'.

These are some of the things you can do.

- Disable podcasts and Ping (iTunes' social network for music lovers) and enable shared libraries (so they can't access your content).
- Specify what age range of music, television shows and apps you want to be accessible – for example, from 12+.

- 'Show content ratings in the library' – this will show you and your child what age ratings the content has been given.
- Restrict anything labelled 'explicit content' – which will include a lot of rap and hip-hop.
- As the administrator, you can set a password and lock your settings, so that your child cannot change anything.
- You can also disable access to the iTunes store altogether.

15

Sharing online

Social networks are obviously the most common places where teenagers 'share' – and that could be anything, from the banal (what the weather is like) to the potentially dangerous (their exact location, or bullying behaviour). But sharing online is not just confined to social networks – it spans the web, in various forms.

Formspring

A flavour of the moment for teenagers is Formspring (another service for over-13s), an increasingly popular question-and-answer site. Launched in 2009, by February 2011 it had over 20 million users, receiving 3.5 million unique visits daily. Each day around 10 million responses to these requests for information are posted.

Members can link their accounts to Facebook and Twitter and the default privacy settings are public. So if you haven't 'protected' your profile, anybody can view the questions you have asked and anybody can answer.

Questions range from the useful ('do you know any good pubs in Glasgow's West End?') to the silly ('do you fancy John?') and the malicious ('how did you get to be so fat?').

More often than not, however, it is used to ask somebody a question you would never ask them in person and it can have devastating consequences, especially for teenagers struggling with self-esteem issues. When asking a question, you can hide your name, meaning anonymous cyber-bullying is extremely easy.

Julia, 15, was a happy-go-lucky girl who set up a Formspring account. A few months later her father passed away and somebody posted this question: "Your dad deserved to die. Why is that?" Unsurprisingly this had a devastating impact on the girl, who needed to have counselling.

In 2010, a 17-year-old New York high school graduate committed suicide after dozens of insulting comments about her had been posted on Formspring.

These two cases highlight the need for parents to understand the sites their teenagers are using, and why it is so important to be kind online.

Of course, Formspring doesn't encourage this behaviour, but with the option of anonymous postings, they are making life easy for cyber-bullies.

Positive uses

As with any new technology, it's how you use it that makes the difference. Sean, 16, used Formspring for a positive reason: "A lot of people use Formspring to get attention, but I used it as a forum to respond to people's negative views about my bisexuality."

People started by asking really rude, offensive questions but he also received some support. Eventually his critics went silent, which Sean puts down to the strong arguments he made in response. Using Formspring in this context could be seen as a positive way to change perceptions.

Like anything online, it's how you use it that counts – and sharing online does not have to be dangerous, if your child understands what's appropriate and what's not.

Do our kids tweet?

Most research shows that teens, and certainly kids, prefer to leave Twitter to us. The looting across UK cities in August 2011 may have changed that. More benignly, teens use Twitter feeds is to keep on top of celebrity gossip.

If your child does choose to tweet, parents should know that Twitter gives its users two settings: make tweets readable to all, or only to a selected group. The same advice applies to Twitter as it does to any other sharing medium on the web.

Blogs

A weblog or 'blog' is an online diary which can be used to share aspects of a person's life or their thoughts or musings on any particular subject, usually something they are passionate about. But should our children be doing this in a public forum? Many experts would argue that the answer to this question is no.

So far we seem to be listening. Just 12% of our children and teenagers are likely to create content for blogs or post an online diary. Many start blogging in their mid to late teens using a platform like Tumblr or WordPress. 'Tumbling' on Tumblr has become particularly popular with teenagers and many are now linking this to their Facebook account.

Blogs are another place where your child should be careful of sharing too much. It could be seen as publicising your diary, and teens may not be fully aware of the implications.

If your teen is blogging, check they're following the guidelines below.

- Make sure your teen thinks about how much they are sharing with the online world, and if they'd want all their friends to read it.
- Check they're not using the blog to be unkind about friends – venting frustration is one thing, but if they are specific, this could be viewed as cyber-bullying (see Chapter 10).
- Be sure that any comments on the blog can be reviewed first by their author.
- Ensure that your teen writes about a past event, rather than their future whereabouts.
- Encourage your teen to use their blog to be creative, and develop their writing skills. This will be a great skill if they want to go into something like journalism later in life, or, for that matter, any job. Being able to express yourself accurately and clearly is an essential skill.
- Make sure your teen's blog shows them in a positive light – and would impress a potential employer. Remember their digital footprint (see p45) may last for years and any silly remarks now may come back to bite them.

> **TIP** Be wary of reading your teen's blog without their permission. Instead, ask whether they would mind you reading out of interest.

Something to encourage?

Although it's mostly teens blogging at the moment, younger children could benefit from starting to blog. The argument is that creativity and passion about a subject are central to the art of blogging, and the technology aspect – which many children love – would encourage them to write more.

As the National Literacy Trust (NLT) points out: "Writing is much more than just an educational issue – it is an essential skill that allows people to participate fully in today's society and to contribute to the economy."[48] In a 2009 survey of over 3,000 children, the NLT found that 75% of children write regularly, usually in digital formats. But given how text-speak is changing the way children write (and spell!), the ability to write grammatically correct sentences with no spelling mistakes will surely become a differentiator as our children enter the job market.

In the age of social media we parents need to teach our children and teenagers to apply common sense at all times. They need to keep their wits about them and think before they sign into a site or post too much information.

This does not mean that they should stop doing everything online, but they do need to be aware that minimising their digital footprint is something they will not live to regret (see p45).

16

The internet is mobile
From smartphones to tablets

As if you did not have enough to worry about with your computers at home, now thrown into the technology mix are smartphones and other lightweight devices known as tablets. If your teenager doesn't have one, you might have one yourself. These make it possible to access the internet at any time and in any place.

There are three main players in this highly competitive and fast-growing arena: Apple (iPhone, iPad), Research in Motion (BlackBerry, PlayBook) and Google (Android devices like the HTC Wildfire, Samsung Galaxy and Motorola Xoom). Less successful have been the Nokia's Symbian and Windows Mobile operating systems and the devices that run on them.

Mobile phones

So popular are mobile phones with our children that research shows that around 70% of UK children aged five to 16 own a mobile phone, rising to 97% by the time they are 11.[49] Close to one in five children aged five to 15 own a smartphone, but those accessing the internet through their phone are still relatively few as many are on pay-as-you-go and don't have web browsing in place. This is likely to change as contracts become more attractive.

FACT A **smartphone** is both a telephone and a mini-computer rolled into one. Now you can access your email and the internet anywhere – provided of course that there is a wireless connection. It has a more advanced operating system and is able to run the same type of applications you have on your computer.

While Apple's iPhone may have revolutionised the mobile market and is indisputably the most well-known smartphone, our teenagers have helped propel BlackBerry into the mainstream. While the iPhone may be coveted for its music capability, ultimately when it comes to teenagers and their price-sensitive parents, BlackBerry's pricing strategy won the day. The ability to 'BBM' friends – instant messaging using a BlackBerry without eating up text or voice time – has become the ultimate measure of 'coolness' among our teenage text generation.

Still, even BlackBerry does not come cheap and many parents have convinced their children to go for cheaper alternatives. For the moment, pricing structures and payment systems are prohibitive for many parents but it will not be too long before smartphones become more affordable. That may be music to our children's ears but there is a warning bell for us.

New challenges

Mobiles with access to the internet have changed the way we all use technology, but they also bring with them a whole different set of problems.

Many parents buy their children a mobile because it makes them feel their child is contactable and is therefore safer. But this may not be the case. For one, children with smartphones are more likely to get mugged than those without a phone at all – any salesperson at any mobile phone retailer will insist that insurance is essential if you are buying your child a smartphone. Secondly, the ability to access the mobile internet raises a number of new challenges around safety. Your child could start to receive unwanted marketing material; they may be more vulnerable to cyber-bullying; or in a worst-case scenario they might be stalked by a friend or even a stranger they have met online (more on all this later).

Before going any further, ask yourself this.

1. Have you ever read the terms and conditions on any mobile handset you have ever purchased?
2. Do you know that by agreeing to the terms and conditions of that handset, once you access the internet via an unknown network you are giving full permission for your data to be used in any way interested parties see fit?

Chances are that you've never read these terms and conditions and therefore have little idea of how, or where, your data can be used.

"There is a pressing need for better understanding because very few people fully understand the huge power of the device they are holding and that how they use it has both commercial and potential safety implications. If that is true for us as adults, we need to think about what it means for our children."
Mike Hawkes, chairman, Mobile Data Association

Smart settings

Most phones now have access to the internet, and allow users full web access. While it is possible to filter some content at both the network and the device level, parental controls for smartphones and tablets remain fairly limited. Many controls are easy to bypass and parents should remember that inappropriate content can also be sent by text, instant messaging or email to a mobile.

What your network operator can do

All UK mobile network operators offer some degree of parental control for free; however, this is usually not automatically turned on. Here are a few of the biggest operators and the services they provide.

- T-Mobile's Content Lock helps prevent children from accessing 18-rated material and has three settings: on, moderate and off.
- O2's parental control service limits the websites children can use on their mobiles; only sites that have been classified as suitable and interesting for children under 12 can be accessed.
- Vodafone's Content Control is applied to all phones, if the age of the user has not been confirmed. You have to register that you are over 18 for this to be turned off.
- On the 3 network, you have to enter the addresses of the websites you want blocked, or which use particular words – this means it blacklists websites, which isn't the most thorough filtering tool (see p59).

What the phone or tablet itself can do

Many devices do have some inbuilt controls so you can restrict your child's use. But again, you will have to turn these on as the default settings will almost certainly be open. Each make will be different, and so will each model (new models having better tools, as this issue grows in importance).

Restrictions can include selecting age-appropriate brackets that block unwanted applications and content being shown on the device, disabling geolocation services or password-controlling the ability to download apps. Taking such action can be helpful for younger children who are less likely to undo these. However, when it comes to savvy teenagers, communicating the message about internet safety remains your most powerful tool.

There are three main parental control settings for mobile phones.

- **Content filters** let parents limit what multimedia content their child can download to their phone.
- **Usage controls** help parents control how the child is using a phone, such as by regulating the number of calls and text messages, blocking certain numbers or restricting outgoing calls to a pre-approved list. It may even be possible to disable the phone at certain times.
- **Geolocation controls** are used to monitor a child's whereabouts (see p145).

For the most coveted smartphone, the iPhone, parents can turn off access to explicit content via iTunes, Safari (the browser), YouTube and the ability to buy apps. You can set a four-digit passcode to ensure your child cannot change this. For other devices, it is possible to disable access to the internet completely, but there's not much scope for choosing which websites you can access.

But think before you do this – shutting the internet off altogether might not go down too well – after all, why would your child want a smartphone if they can't access the internet?

TIP Check what safety settings your child's mobile network and device manufacturer can offer you – and be sure to implement these.

Mobile apps

While not all of us may yet have agreed to buy our children their own smartphone, it seems we are happy to hand over our own devices to them for a little peace and quiet. Many parents now download child-friendly games to keep our children busy. Some of these are free; others are available for around 50p or more.

After a number of parents were caught out with huge bills, Apple has introduced a new system which requires a password to be entered before each purchase.[50] The company also responded to concerns about iPhone porn by introducing stronger parental controls.

When buying apps, keep the following in mind.

- Some apps may be free but before long your child will be encouraged to upgrade.
- Make sure the applications your child is playing are age-appropriate – there are some very good educational ones out there.
- Don't give your child your password, and don't store it in your phone (or theirs). That way, they can't buy apps without your knowledge.

TIP   Check out www.funeducationalapps.com or www. bestkidsapps.com for recommendations of fun and safe apps.

Safety apps

As Apple's marketing gurus will have us believe, there is an app for everything. But is it true? Most software providers have branched into the world of smartphone apps – this is a fast-growing market – and some are now providing safety software for mobiles, but the bottom line is that these products are even more limited than those available for PCs.

Safe Eyes (iPhone) and Security Shield (BlackBerry, Symbian, Windows Mobile and Android devices) were the two main apps tested by the European Commission's ongoing SIP study. It found that while there may be many parental control tools for mobile phones, only a few – at the time of going to press – were able to filter webpage content; they seem to focus more on traditional phone-related activities like texting.

Still, installing one of these (see Chapter 8) may add some peace of mind and additional control. Yet again, it is still relatively early days in the world of smartphones, and you can be sure there will be many more additions to security and safety settings in the future.

With the launch of every new operating system or device, parental controls will evolve and hopefully improve. This is a priority for the UK Government and it is up to parents to check with the phone retailer and their network operator what the options for protection are.

Geolocation technology – super cool or super scary?

Mike Hawkes, chairman of the Mobile Data Association, is passionate about consumer protection and the need to get the right systems in place so that the use of mobile technology can really benefit us. He has worked closely with numerous police agencies and the UK Government on how to keep children safe and spends a good deal of time playing with mobile devices, to establish exactly what is possible.

More often than not, the level of detailed personal information he is able to access about a person and their exact whereabouts using standard mobile services surprises even him. This he says is down to geolocation technology.

In simple terms geolocation technology reveals the exact location of another person who is using the internet.

Many parents will have heard about geolocation technology because it has been touted as a way for worried parents to track their children when they are out and about.

You've probably used it yourself: it's the same technology that works satellite navigators – using either global positioning satellites or nearby mobile base stations to determine your location and make getting to an unknown destination stress-free.

Geolocation technology is a marketing person's dream. With geolocation, it is possible to target people – and increasingly children – with the things they might want, available in the location they are in, in a much more detailed way. Services like Facebook Places, Foursquare and Gowalla enable users to find places they might like in areas they are in.

> FACT Most smartphones and digital cameras geo-tag photographs automatically. So when these are uploaded to the internet, the exact location of where a photograph is taken can be established down to within a few feet.

With a little imagination it is easy to see how this technology could prove problematic. In short, geotechnology makes stalking possible and also pretty easy to do.

It also brings a whole new dimension to identity theft, which is a growing concern in the UK. With a few very standard applications you can very quickly build a picture of a person's life, location, likes and dislikes.

So while geotechnology can bring parents peace of mind, as with other new technologies, we need to safeguard against misuse. Decide for yourself whether the risks outweigh the positives and talk to your child about how this technology is being used.

It is possible to turn off geolocation technology. Go to the settings on your phone, and you should find location settings or services, which you can change. For some devices you can only turn this off globally, for all applications on the phone; others let you choose to only turn off geo-tagging of photos.

The rise of abuse by mobile

Abuse in its different forms is made much easier by mobile phones. We covered cyber-bullying in detail in Chapter 10, and mobile phones are a prime cyber-bullying tool.

If your child is being victimised by mobile phone it is essential that they keep a record of all communication. A report can only be taken seriously if there is evidence.

Another very worrying trend is the rise in 'sexting' by minors. As the name implies, 'sexting' is when somebody sends a sexually explicit, often unsolicited, message or photograph, usually from one mobile phone to another.

FACT According to EU Kids Online, 12% of children have seen or received a sexual message.[51] Interestingly, the research also shows that far fewer children admit to sending or posting sexual messages and the majority do not seem particularly affected by the experience.

Whether they are affected or not, teenagers should be aware that in the UK it is illegal to produce, own or disseminate or share photos of an explicit nature of anyone under the age of 18. Even if both parties involved are teenagers and both consented, both parties could find themselves in trouble. When sexual images are used for bullying, blackmail or child abuse, legal prosecutions become increasingly likely.

> ### Risqué and risky
>
> Tom, 16, had taken some rather risqué photographs of his girlfriend, Andrea, which she had naively agreed to when things were going well with them.
>
> Then their relationship hit a rocky patch and one afternoon, really annoyed by something she had said, Tom sent one of these photographs on to his friend Jack. As a joke, Jack forwarded the photograph on to his contacts list and before long the photograph was tagged on Facebook, where hundreds of people had access to it.
>
> Unsurprisingly, Tom was soon an ex-boyfriend and not long after the police turned up at his house. Andrea had told her parents and together they had reported the incident to the police. Because Andrea was a minor, her ex-boyfriend and anybody who had shared the photograph were liable for prosecution.

The good news for parents is that mobile network operators are working hard to protect users and provide them with information about safe use. The problem is when you get to the shop floor only to find that the salesperson has not been properly trained. The information is available but the onus is on you the parent to ask for it.

Each mobile operator is also very different, so do some research into what each can offer you in terms of safety and privacy. The following advice is compiled from Childnet International and the Mobile Data Association.

Checklist when buying a mobile for your child

1. **Safety services** – find out what services are available to keep your child safe on their mobile.
2. **Filters for internet access** – if the phone has internet access, find out what filters are available to block potentially harmful content. If the filter is switched off, ask the salesperson to turn it on.

3. **Privacy** – quite often privacy settings on a mobile phone need to be activated. Make sure privacy settings are switched on. If you cannot do this, ask the salesperson to show you how.

4. **Age range** – establish whether the phone is registered for a child or adult user. Keep your credit card number away from your child, as most operators will change the age rating if they receive a request from a user who can provide a valid credit card number. Most operators treat credit cards as proof of age.

5. **Getting a new number** – find out if it is possible to change a mobile number for free. In the event of your child being cyber-bullied this may come in handy.

6. **Bluetooth-enabled phones** – bluetooth is a technology which allows phones to 'talk' to other phones which have the same technology and are in the same vicinity. As such, your child could receive unwanted messages, and personal information on the phone could be at risk. Ask the salesperson if the phone you are buying has this technology and ask them to set it in the safest possible way for a child user.

> TIP Emphasise the importance of leaving Bluetooth switched off whenever not in use. Children transfer data by Bluetooth all the time – get them used to switching off when they have finished with it.

7. **Premium rate numbers** (the ones that start with 09 or four- or five-digit codes like 0871) – you do not want your teenager racking up huge phone bills after phoning an X-rated number, so find out if you can bar calls to these numbers. If it is not possible to bar these numbers find out what protection they offer for users.

8. **IM services** – some mobile devices have instant messaging services like BlackBerry Messenger (BBM) and iMessenger. Chat is not moderated in these devices as it's just like sending a stream, but some types have the option of separate chat rooms. Find out if there are any restrictions on these.

9. **Nuisance or malicious calls or texts** – what is your mobile operator's policy regarding these? They should have systems and procedures in place. In the light of rising numbers of 'sexts' being received by minors it is worth finding out what your mobile operator will do to address this and other nuisance calls. If your child receives one you should report it and the operator should take action.

10. **Spam** – operators should take action against spam. Find out what their policy is and where to report abuse. If you get marketing text messages and want to stop them appearing on the handset, reply with 'STOP' or 'STOP ALL' as marketing companies have a legal obligation to provide this opt-out mechanism. This should also apply to premium rate messaging services.

TIP Switch off international roaming (or ask the store to do this for you). If your child travels overseas and accesses the internet via the mobile network operator, you may receive a hefty bill. Note that wifi systems do not use the mobile networks and, while less secure, a wifi hotspot will provide access to the internet without incurring additional data roaming charges.

As parents we should be asking for far more from the companies that are likely to pocket our hard-earned cash than just cheaper products and payment pricing models. There is no doubt that mobile computing poses some real challenges and this is not something we should be complacent about.

Tablets and hand-held devices

In airports and cafes, on buses and trains, slim, light and easy-to-handle tablets are increasingly becoming the norm. Popular for game playing, these devices may become a growing concern for parents.

In 2011, a tiny percentage of children (under 2%) accessed the internet on tablets.[52] While this doesn't seem like a major problem yet, tablets like the iPad are rapidly becoming trendy, as are devices like the BlackBerry PlayBook and Motorola Xoom.

Apple's iPad is the most popular tablet device but Research in Motion, the company behind the BlackBerry mobile, is hoping that its PlayBook will gain popularity among its teenage mobile users.

When it comes to the PlayBook and other Android devices there is very limited parental control software, if any, at the moment.

Apple is a bit of a step ahead and, like the iPhone, the iPad offers some general safety restrictions which make it suitable for the whole family's use. But it's all or nothing – you have to apply the restrictions and then live with them as well.

- You can block the internet altogether, or block specific websites like YouTube or iTunes.
- For browsing, select SafeSearch (as you have done for your PC) on Google, Yahoo! and the like (see p125).
- As with mobiles, you can disable geotechnology through the location settings.
- You can restrict the type of content purchased for applications, music and podcasts by age ratings.
- You can't actually set restrictions on YouTube from an iPad, like you can from a PC (see p129), so the best thing might be to block this site altogether.
- Set a passcode for your iPad so that your child can't use it without your knowledge.

> **TIP** New operating systems, devices and software are being released constantly, so we have not been too specific in our instructions, while still giving you practical and helpful information.

Part 4

The future

The dilemma of how to keep our children safe online has undoubtedly hit mainstream discourse. Looking to the future, there can be little doubt that online safety will remain a hot topic while we as a society continue to grapple with how the internet, still a child itself, has changed our lives forever.

One thing is certain: change will continue.

> *"Everybody knows that the current regime is not stable and is not sustainable in the long run because it is founded on a fiction, which is that age-related statements on websites mean something when plainly they don't."*
> **John Carr, adviser to the UK Government and United Nations on child online safety**

There is a lot we do not know and it will take at least a generation before some issues are fully understood. Is the internet really changing the way our brains work? Will our children really think differently from us because of their early access to technology? Will being exposed to pornography affect our children's ability to form meaningful sexual relationships? Are those who have been given free rein to play video games likely to have the edge in the technology job market over the children whose parents controlled their screen time? Will future societies be run by narcissistic, impulsive and amoral beings who have become so intoxicated by the power of the internet that their e-personality now reflects the one they have created in the real world? Or will we, perhaps, see demand returning for traditional skills like stone masonry, wood carving and sewing?

As we ponder these questions, government bodies are considering their role in protecting our young people. For example, improving parental control over age-restricted material on the internet was the recommendation from Mothers' Union chief executive Reg Bailey in his review[53] of the commercialisation and sexualisation of childhood. Whether this happens via government regulation or industry co-operation, one of the main considerations will be establishing what duty of care is necessary for the vulnerable in our society and whether the price the average person needs to pay for this will limit the enormous benefits of the internet for everybody else. Being unsure of how to keep all the relevant stakeholders happy – big business, social workers, psychologists, teachers, parents and children – will likely lead to a lot more research and many more reports.

Industry providers from all corners of the sector will continue to think of ways to maximise profits in a highly competitive industry – keeping our children safe will be one way of doing that. Charities like Childnet International will, finances permitting, keep doing their excellent work in educating parents, children and teachers. And schools will hopefully continue to revise and rethink how to educate our children in the 21st century against the backdrop of tight budgets.

What about parents? What should we be demanding for our children from government, the industry and educators? And what should we be demanding from technology?

Let us consider two important questions.

1. What more can be done to protect our children online?
2. How best do we equip our children for the 21st century?

17

What more can be done?

As parents we must demand more from the technology companies that are captivating our children with new products, games and social media. It is only through pressure brought to bear by civil society that governments listen and companies are ultimately forced to change.

This is what happened in the gambling world.

> "For all their fine words of how they were doing their best to protect children, most of the gambling industry did absolutely nothing until it was a legal requirement for them to verify the age of users on their websites."
> **John Carr, adviser to the UK Government and United Nations on child online safety**

Some companies will do it better and faster than others, recognising that good business practice will ultimately give them an edge and build an all-important relationship of trust.

There are a number of high-level debates currently under way which we can become involved in. How the digital world can potentially compromise our children's privacy is one that is gathering force. "This is particularly important when you consider the rise of geolocation-based services," says David Miles, director, Europe, Middle East and Africa for FOSI (see p145).

Another hot topic is whether age verification systems are a good idea. Given that as many as 25% of UK children aged eight to 12 subscribe to websites that give 13 as a minimum age, this is a really important issue and one we should become involved in.

How would age verification systems work?

Before you start panicking about identity theft, new identity technologies need not compromise privacy – they could be something as simple as a machine-readable digital token containing the bare minimum of information and would not be required for all areas of the internet, only for age-restricted sites.

Germany, for example, has introduced a mandatory chip and pin system for accessing adult content and many other countries are looking at possible solutions to address the issue.

Sound good? As ever, these things are never straightforward and would require a huge amount of effort, invention and, of course, money. Databases could be constructed by governments or individual companies. Proof of identity could be called for when registering for a service, along the lines of a passport application process. One suggestion is that this could happen via the school's existing IT system and/or by the parent registering their child with a third-party vendor. Keeping information accurate and updated would be the responsibility of the vendor, which would work closely with schools. Only schools and these companies would have access to the details, rather than the website, which is currently the case. The exception would be in police cases where officers could be sent to the school with the child's ID to investigate. Websites would be vetted and periodically checked by various regulatory bodies to ensure compliance.

Children would be given a security ID to register on approved sites. The default setting would be no marketing and parents would be given the option to receive a newsletter of offers.

Will they work?

In theory, yes, but there are plenty of opponents. The argument goes that by introducing third-party vendors our children's data will be at even greater risk than it is now.

> "How do you know what they are going to do with the data, where they are going to store it and so on? There should be greater emphasis on the company you are dealing with taking more control of data protection."
> **Christopher Boyd, senior threat researcher, GFI Software**

> "There are so many shades of disagreement, so many assumptions and perspectives here, that it will be very difficult to agree a standard."
> **Dr Shirley Atkinson, lecturer in information systems and e-safety expert in mathematics and computing, Plymouth University**

Four things parents can do now

1. Call for greater responsibility from retailers selling age-restricted products to children.
2. Put pressure on companies to introduce stronger measures for verifying the age of children signing up to their websites.

3. Call for greater debate around age verification and what systems are available.
4. Report criminal abuse to an organisation like the Internet Watch Foundation (www.iwf.org.uk).

Whatever happens, nothing can ever replace ongoing education and the need for us parents to keep communicating with our children.

18

Media literacy
Equipping our children
for the 21st century

Many educators now hold the view that they have to move with the times and embrace the internet and especially social networking platforms as educational tools.

One company that has been researching this is DigitalME, a company exploring and promoting new directions in learning, which is backed by the British Council among others.

> "The dilemma facing schools is that the skills that are
> easiest to teach are also the ones that are easiest to digitise,
> automate and outsource."
> **Tim Riches, chief executive, DigitalME**

So if this is the dilemma facing schools, what does it mean for parents? We need to take a more active interest in our children's use of technology. If we don't, there will be a growing divide between those children whose parents are unaware of or uninterested in their education, and those who are actively engaging and taking a real interest.

An important component of this will be staying safe, but getting involved in their digital media literacy is just as important. Media studies used to be viewed as a flaky subject, but it is now essential to our children's future. Navigating the web effectively, knowing how to assess the authenticity of content, the ability to sift and make sense of vast quantities of material are all skills our children will need.

Some of the UK's leading minds are currently examining the future of education in a digital world. How can social networks or mobile phones be harnessed as an educational tool? Should there be greater emphasis on project-based learning where children are required to use all the key skills – communication, collaboration, presentation, accessing experts, creating, editing and so on – to build a project over a whole term?

As parents, then, we need to rethink the things we restrict and the things we encourage. For example, some parents may feel uncomfortable about young children blogging. But is this a mistake when some studies have found that children who blog have higher levels of literacy than those who do not? (See p138).

Finding the right balance between technology and social skills will be central, and creativity is an important part of this.

> "Given the rate of progress of computing power and the science and maths education in China and India, creativity will be the greatest differentiator by the time my girls start working."
> **Rob, technology consultant and dad to Hanna (7) and Leah (5)**

All too often we hear that our children know more than us and are more technology-literate than us. In academic circles the term 'digital native' has been used to describe the generation of children who have grown up with digital technology – the first of whom have just come of age. The theory goes that children, because they have grown up with technology, inherently know how to use it, unlike their parents who could be defined as 'digital immigrants'.

But in the UK, this notion of children as 'digital natives' and their parents as disadvantaged 'digital immigrants' is one that is increasingly being dismissed.

> *"Our children may look like so-called 'digital natives' whizzing around websites, but many still find it difficult to get to the information they need."*
> **Tim Riches, chief executive, DigitalME**

> *"I absolutely think the 'digital natives' idea is a myth and that campaigns and initiatives [for parents and children] are proving effective."*
> **Professor Sonia Livingstone, EU Kids Online network,[54] London School of Economics**

> *"Children may inherently be able to push the right buttons but parents are experts in life and can assess something based on previous experience and wisdom."*
> **Dr Shirley Atkinson, lecturer in information systems and e-safety expert in mathematics and computing, Plymouth University**

This debate will probably continue until there are no digital immigrants left to discuss this dichotomy.

One of the biggest risks our children face is that they will end up on the wrong side of the digital divide. So using our wisdom and understanding to direct our children safely, successfully and responsibly through the digital age will be one of the most important things we do.

The last word

In spring 2011, BBC Radio 4 broadcast a series of talks about the Christian season of Lent. One of these was given by Imam Feisal Abdul Rauf, the chairman of the Cordoba Initiative Islamic Cultural Centre, near 'Ground Zero' in New York. During the course of the programme he stated: "We have to bring up our children for a time different to our own." He was reflecting on the conflict between faith and identity but could just have easily have been talking about children growing up with technology.

But while UK families grapple with the challenges of new technologies and the internet, we should not forget the culture shock that online content represents to countries outside the developed world.

> "The cultural inappropriateness of content in cultures and among faiths in the developing world can be even more profound. Their ability to deal with the risks is often constrained by bigger socio-economic priorities like poverty, disease or lack of electricity. It is also sometimes important to remember that the global impact and opportunities of technology are profound and lasting, only for those who have access to it."
> **David Miles, director, Europe, Middle East and Africa, FOSI**

It is a truism that we have to bring up our children for a time different to our own. This is certainly not easy, but perhaps one day our children will look back with amusement at how we worried about their online life in the first two decades of the 21st century. After all, just about every technology causes somebody to fret about the moral downfall of society: think of Mary Whitehouse and the Clean Up TV campaign of 1964.

The last word

In concluding, my hope is that you'll take the following with you.

1. Keep lines of communication open and the discussion straightforward and honest.
2. Understand the risks but don't overreact.
3. Investigate parental control tools and install what is appropriate according to the age of your child.
4. Know what services your children may be using or wish to use and show an interest in these.
5. Think carefully about whether your children really need every single new device that is launched – not only is excessive consumerism a growing problem, the environment matters too.
6. Become an activist for online safety – and bring it to the forefront of your family's and school's agendas.

Enjoy the journey.

Glossary

We've included some of the less well-known words you'll come across in the book or online.

3G or third generation: a standard for a mobile phone network that offers fast connections allowing users to connect to the internet, video call or watch films

Adware: software that has adverts embedded in it. Not necessarily harmful but can be integrated with spyware

Applications or apps: software programs that can run on a computer, phone or other electronic device.

Block: to prevent a program or website from being reached by a person or to stop another person from contacting you in, for example, a chat room

Browser: a program, like Microsoft Explorer, Firefox and Safari, that allows you to access the worldwide web

Buddy: an online friend; usually a person who you communicate with using instant messaging or chat programs and who you have in your buddy list

CEOP: Child Exploitation and Online Protection Centre, now part of the National Crime Agency

Cookie: a small file that is stored on the user's computer which is read by the server each time the user revisits the same website. This helps to keep track of personal preferences, shopping choices and so on and can be used for marketing

Data: information stored on a computer

Glossary

File sharing: copying files over the internet. Usually the files contain music, films or programs, but any sort of file can be shared

Filter: a way to prevent certain types of material, particularly harmful ones, from reaching your computer. Limits access to content or material on the internet by installing software or by altering settings in a web browser to restrict access to certain websites, bad language and so on

Fraping: when somebody hacks into your Facebook account and posts something embarrassing or rude

Global Positioning System (GPS): a mobile system using satellites to provide information of where you are and when; accurate to within about 10 metres

IM (instant messaging): allows friends to communicate electronically using text messages in real time

IP (internet protocol) address: each internet-connected computer or device is assigned a unique number known as an IP address. A bit like a telephone number, it is usually coded by country so if the need arises it can be used to identify where a connection to the internet has been made

Malware: malicious software that can damage your computer, including viruses, apps that steal your personal information (spyware), unwanted adverts (adware) or programs that make a computer vulnerable to hackers (Trojan horses)

Moderation (of chat rooms or other services): when there is adult supervision and/or a technical solution that will pick up offensive language or anything that may be considered inappropriate, such as disclosing personal information

Network: interconnected computers linked together to exchange data

P2P or peer-to-peer: P2P networks allow users to share files on their computer with people anywhere; otherwise known as file sharing

Parental control software: a program that adults install to filter and monitor use and access of sites. It can restrict access to certain sites, block some, keep a record of time spent online and so on

Phishing: an attempt to trick people into visiting malicious websites by sending emails or other messages purporting to come from banks or online shops. The emails have links in them which take people to fake sites set up to look like the real thing, where passwords and account details can be stolen

Platform: a computer system that includes hardware of some sort and allows software to run

Portal: like a door to other parts of the internet, a website that pulls together sources from all over the web

Security updates: changes to existing programs which identify and fix problems. Some require a user to download them; others happen in real time

Skype: a program that lets you make phone calls, with video, to other users over the internet for free (unless you wish to call a landline or mobile)

Social network(ing): websites or other channels which build online communities of people who can share interests, set up groups, upload content and interact in a number of ways using, for example, email, chat or bulletin boards

Spyware: software developed to steal your personal information

Trojan horse: software that pretends to be a useful program like a word processor but really installs spyware or adware or opens up your computer to hackers

Virtual learning environment (VLE): a school-based network of programs and data to support teaching and learning, which children can access at home. Also known as managed learning environment (MLE)

Virus: a computer program that copies itself and infects a computer, spreading from one computer to another

Web 2.0: term given to define the second generation of the internet, encompassing developments like blogs and social networks

Worm: a self-replicating malware which copies to other computers on the network without any user intervention

Useful resources

Sources used in the book

The Bailey Review (www.education.gov.uk/b0074315/bailey-review)
The Byron Review Action Plan, June 2008 (www.education.gov.uk/
publications/standard/publicationdetail/page1/DCSF-00521-2008)
CEOP: *Annual Review 2010–11* (www.ceop.police.uk)
CEOP: *Strategic Overview 2009–10* (www.ceop.police.uk)
CHILDWISE: *The Monitor Report 2010–11* (www.childwise.co.uk)
EU Kids Online network funded by the European Commission
Safer Internet Programme, (project code SIP-KEP-321803,
www.eukidsonline.net)
Ofcom: *UK children's media literacy*, April 2011 (www.ofcom.org.uk)
Family Online Safety Institute (www.fosi.org)

General advice and reporting abuse

CEOP Think U Know: www.thinkuknow.co.uk
Childnet International: www.childnet.com
Digizen: www.digizen.org
Family Online Safety Institute: www.fosi.org
Internet Watch Foundation: www.iwf.org.uk
KidSMART: www.kidsmart.org.uk
UK Safer Internet Centre: www.saferinternet.org.uk

Cyber-bullying resources

Act Against Bullying: www.actagainstbullying.com
Beatbullying: www.beatbullying.org
CyberMentors: www.cybermentors.org.uk
Bullying.org: www.bullying.org
Kidscape: www.kidscape.org.uk
A useful film, *Let's Fight it Together*, can be found at old.digizen.org/
cyberbullying/fullfilm.aspx

Child-friendly search engines

Ask Kids: www.askkids.com
KidsClick!: www.kidsclick.org
KidZui: www.kidzui.com
Yahoo! for Kids: kids.yahoo.com

Educational tools

BBC Bitesize: www.bbc.co.uk/schools/bitesize
DigitalME: www.digitalme.co.uk
Free Writing Center: www.freewritingcenter.com

Mobile help

Ofcom: parental controls for mobile phones: consumers.ofcom.org.uk

Parental control tools reviews

European Commission Safer Internet Programme benchmarking:
www.yprt.eu/sip
Filtra: www.filtra.info
Parental controls reviews: getparentalcontrols.org

Other useful websites offering reviews of age-appropriate games and how-to guides

Common Sense Media: www.commonsensemedia.org – useful for
rating games
Facebook for Parents: www.facebookforparents.org
Get Safe Online: www.getsafeonline.org
John Carr's blog (adviser to the UK Government and United Nations
on child online safety): johnc1912.wordpress.com

The Online Mom: www.theonlinemom.com
Parenting section on Your Sphere: www.internet-safety.yoursphere.com
Facebook safety: www.facebook.com/safety

Endnotes

Introduction

1. EU Kids Online network funded by the European Commission (DG Information Society) Safer Internet Programme: www.eukidsonline.net

Introduction to Part 1

2. www.fosi.org/downloads/resources/fosi-kids-tips.pdf

Chapter 1

3. *Strategic Overview 2009 10*, CEOP
4. www.bbc.co.uk/health/physical_health/child_development/safety_road.shtml
5. www.bbc.co.uk/news/technology-10953600
6. *Strategic Overview 2009–10*, CEOP, p9
7. *CHILDWISE Monitor Special Report 2010: Digital Lives*, CHILDWISE
8. www.drlinda.co.uk/pdfs/sexualisation_review.pdf
9. EU Kids Online network, pp26–27
10. Peter, J. & Valkenburg, P. M. (in press). Processes Underlying the Effects of Adolescents' Use of Sexually Explicit Internet Material: The role of perceived realism. Communication Research.

Chapter 2

11. *Annual Review 2010–11*, CEOP
12. *Strategic Overview 2009–10*, CEOP
13. EU Kids Online UK report, p36

Chapter 3

14. *UK children's media literacy*, Ofcom, 2011: stakeholders.ofcom.org.uk/binaries/research/media-literacy/media-lit11/childrens.pdf
15. Norton cybercrime statistics, September 2010

Chapter 4

16. *CHILDWISE Monitor Special Report 2010: Digital Lives*, CHILDWISE
17. www.bioinitiative.org/report

Chapter 5

18. EU Kids Online
19. Gleave, J. (2009), *Children's Time to Play: A literature review*, NCB for Play England

Chapter 6

20. EU Kids Online II
21. *UK children's media literacy*, Ofcom, 2011
22. EU Kids Online II
23. *UK children's media literacy*, Ofcom, 2011
24. EU Kids Online II
25. EU Kids Online II
26. UK children's media literacy, Ofcom

Chapter 7

27. *The Monitor Report 2010–11*, CHILDWISE
28. www.bris.ac.uk/news/2010/7235.html
29. www.sciencedaily.com/releases/2011/04/110420164419.htm
30. Family Online Safety Institute (www.fosi.org)
31. EU Kids Online II

Chapter 8

32. EU Kids Online II
33. ec.europa.eu/information_society/activities/sip/docs/sip_bench2_results/report_feb11.pdf

Chapter 9

34. EU Kids Online II
35. www.tes.co.uk/article.aspx?storycode=6033403

Chapter 10

36. Digizen, a Childnet International programme: www.digizen.org/downloads/CYBERBULLYING.pdf
37. Harris Interactive: Trends & Tudes: www.ncpc.org/resources/files/pdf/bullying/Cyberbullying%20Trends%20-%20Tudes.pdf

Chapter 11

38. *The Monitor Report 2010–11* and *CHILDWISE Monitor Special Report 2010: Digital Lives*, CHILDWISE
39. EU Kids Online II

Chapter 12

40. EU Kids Online II
41. *UK children's media literacy*, Ofcom, 2011 and Amaze Generation study
42. news.bbc.co.uk/1/hi/7094764.stm
43. Griffiths, M.D., 'Online computer gaming: Advice for parents and teachers', *Education and Health*, vol. 27, no. 1, pp3–6
44. www.bbc.co.uk/blogs/knowledgeexchange/westminsterone.pdf

Chapter 13

45. EU Kids Online II

Chapter 14

46. EU Kids Online II
47. EU Kids Online II

Chapter 15

48. www.literacytrust.org.uk/research/nlt_research/261_young_peoples_writing_attitudes_behaviour_and_the_role_of_technology

Chapter 16

49. *CHILDWISE Monitor Special Report 2010: Digital Lives*, CHILDWISE
50. www.bbc.co.uk/blogs/watchdog/2010/09/iphone_apps.html
51. EU Kids Online II
52. *UK children's media literacy*, Ofcom, 2011

Introduction to Part 4

53. www.education.gov.uk/b0074315/bailey-review

Chapter 18

54. www.eukidsonline.net